WEAPONS OF RIGHTEOUSNESS

Building Strong Christians for the Battle

Closing Spiritual Doorways
STUDY GUIDE

GIL STIEGLITZ

www.ptlb.com

Weapons of Righteousness Series
Building Strong Christians for the Battle
Closing Spiritual Doorways Study Guide

© 2014, 2018 Gil Stieglitz

Published by PTLB Publishing, Roseville, California, 95661
www.ptlb.com

Cover by John Chase
Copyedited by Jennifer Edwards
Book design by Kelly Stuber

ISBN:978-0-9968855-6-0

Religion: Christian Life/Spiritual Warfare
Religion: Christian Ministry/Discipleship
Religion: Christian Ministry/Pastoral Resources

All rights reserved. No part of this publication may be reproduced, stored in a retrieval system, or transmitted in any way by any means-electronic, mechanical, photocopy, recording, or otherwise-without the prior permission of the copyright holder, except as provided by USA copyright law.

All Scripture verses are from the New American Standard Bible unless otherwise indicated.
New American Standard Bible: 1995 update.
1995 La Habra, CA: The Lockman Foundation.

Printed in the United States of America

CONTENTS

Series Introduction 5
The Seven Spiritual Doorways 13

Closing the Doorway of Pride 23
Overcoming Pride and Moving to a Place of Humility ... 25

Closing the Doorway of Rebellion 37
Turning Rebellion into Appropriate Submission 39

Closing the Doorway of Bitterness 47
Turning Bitterness into a Forgiving Heart 49

Closing the Doorway of Lust 63
Overcoming Lust and Developing a Pure Heart 65
Meditating on Scripture to Overcome Temptation 75

Closing the Doorway of Anger 83
Turning Anger into a Controlled Soul 85

Closing the Doorway of Occult Practices 97
Turning Occult Involvement
   into Worship of God Alone 99
Ridding Your House of Occult Objects 106
Discontinuing Occult Practices 113

Closing the Doorway of Transference 123
Turning Transference into Spiritual Freedom 125
Assessing Spiritual and Moral History 133
Fighting Victimization 149
Breaking Curses 155

Conclusion 161

How to Use This Book 163
About the Author 173
More Resources from Principles to Live By 174

SERIES INTRODUCTION

During the first three hundred years of the Christian Church, individual Christians and the Church itself were a dynamic force. In spite of hostile spiritual, religious, and governmental forces raised up against it, the Christian Church changed the world. People flocked to the god Christianity worshipped because the idea of having a personal relationship with the one true God was overwhelming. Plus, it was the only religion where they could be permanently liberated from the spirits, temptations, and wickedness of the ancient world.

The early church trained Christians to know God and how to use all the weapons of righteousness that the Lord Jesus Christ provided. Equipped with the dozens of spiritual weapons written about in the Scriptures, average Christians were able to create a life of freedom, dignity, love, and joy, which was unknown in the ancient world. These "weapons of righteousness" allowed them to build a spiritual force field around their life, which shielded them from the wickedness around them. They were in the world, but they were not of it. They knew they were in a spiritual war, and they were ready for it. They not only survived, but they thrived in the midst of exactly the kind of wickedness that infects our societies today. With teaching and practice, they learned and became proficient with these weapons of righteousness in their churches. During those first three hundred years, it was these small, simple churches that were the places, the spiritual schools, where Christians became fully equipped to live a different kind of life—not through a seminary, university, or graduate course.

Unfortunately, the modern church is only now beginning to acknowledge the spiritual nature of the war with sin and evil. There is not yet in our churches acknowledgment of the need for spiritual battle training, let alone consistent training systems for Christians to become fully equipped to fight against them. It's almost as if we are fighting the enemy with one hand tied behind our backs. The study guides in the Weapons of Righteousness Series attempts to reintroduce the Christian Church to the righteous weapons that Jesus and the apostles tell us about in the New Testament. As Christians become thoroughly equipped with these weapons, individuals will be freed completely and the church dynamic again. With great anticipation and hope, I have watched numerous individuals, churches, and organizations begin to speak into the spiritual war we all face. But we need a more systematic and practical form of training.

These study guides outline forty different "weapons systems" with individual weapons for creating a righteous life of love, joy, and spiritual power. They outline each weapon and give practical spiritual workouts to learn how to use them effectively. Each Christian and each church should plan to dive deeper into these weapons systems to cement their understanding. My hope is that these study guides will offer a template to unleash other creative projects that will release the power of Christ in Christians and in His bride, the Church.

Spiritual Warfare

Everyone is living in the midst of spiritual warfare. It's all around us. But people are confused about what spiritual warfare actually is, so let me define it for you. Certainly, at times, it may involve cases of demons inhabiting a person's body, but this is in extreme cases. The primary arenas of spiritual warfare are actually in our thoughts, choices, emotions, and actions. It consists of thoughts to do evil that fly through our minds, or choices that suggest themselves to us even though we know they are wrong. It is the emotions of fear, despair, anger, depression, and hatred that seek to overwhelm us, keeping us from doing God's ideal. Each of these can be likened to bullets, arrows, and explosives of a spiritual war.

As in a battle, we need protection and the ability to fight back. Fortunately for us, God has graciously given us a huge cache of spiritual weapons to push back the darkness. Some of these weapons protect us from the attacks of the enemy, and some create new levels of spiritual calm in our life.

The number one goal of life for a Christian is to love God, love others, and love one's self in a righteous way. (Matt 22:37-39) The Devil's number one goal is to prevent real love from happening or pervert it into something destructive. Over the last thirty-plus years, the church as a whole has been turning out incredibly weak Christians. This book is an attempt to change that. We need Christians who know how to live out their faith with weapons at the ready. If injustice is to be corrected, we need fully developed Christians who understand and are skilled with the weapons of righteousness.

It is clear that evil is growing. Injustice, abuse, and oppression are everywhere. The apostle Paul faced a whole world full of every kind of injustice and oppression, just like we do today (political, religious, occupational, mental, emotional). How do we become stronger to make a difference? Tucked away in a little verse written to the Corinthians is God's answer. Second Corinthians 6:7 says, "...in the word of truth, in the power of God; by the weapons of righteousness for the right hand and the left..." God's answer is to become equipped with the weapons of righteousness.

I have been involved in helping people grapple with all levels of spiritual warfare, from simple temptation, to severe demon oppression. In every case, the weapons that Christ has given us are adequate when we use them. As I have helped hundreds of people deepen their faith, prepare for ministry, and escape from the clutches of the Devil, it is these weapons of righteousness that have carried the day. I offer these study guides as a practical overview on these weapons systems. We must regularly ask the question: If we become effective at this, who wins and who loses? If your answer is everyone except the wicked wins, then proceed.

Other Books in This Series

1. The Spiritual Disciplines
2. The Ten Foundational Doctrines of Christianity
3. Basic Spiritual Warfare: The Three Enemies and the Four Weapons
4. Closing Spiritual Doorways
5. The Armor of God
6. The Beatitudes: Christ-like Behavior
7. God the Father: The Five Aspects of God
8. The Lord Jesus Christ: His Life, Death, and Resurrection
9. The Present Ministries of the Lord Jesus Christ
10. Knowing the Schemes of the Devil
11. The Holy Spirit: Empowering Believers through Various Ministries
12. The Fruits of the Spirit
13. The Gifts of the Spirit
14. The Present Ministries of the Holy Spirit
15. The Bible

16. Salvation: We are Saved to Qualify and be Empowered to Love God, Others, and Ourselves in a Righteous Manner

17. The Afterlife: Judgment Day, Heaven, and Hell

18. Biblical Meditation

19. Holy Angels

20. Testing: The Fruit, the Content, the Spirit

21. Great Commandments

22. The Boundaries of Love for You and Others (Ten Commandments)

23. A Loving, Righteous Husband

24. A Loving, Righteous Wife

25. A Loving, Righteous Marriage

26. A Maximized, Righteous Individual

27. A Loving, Righteous Family EPIC Parents—Five "R" Kids

28. A Righteous Business

29. A Gracious, Ethical Employee

30. Righteously Earning, Handling, and Generosity with Money

31. A Supportive Community of True, Ethical Friends

32. God's Radical Plan to Turn Enemies into Friends

33. A Vibrant, Growing, and Healthy Church

34. A Just, Loving, and Righteous Society

35. Prayer: 39 Different Ways

36. Godly Wisdom: The Triple-Win and Proverbs

37. Margin: Rest and Sabbath

38. Christian Deliverance: Methods and Techniques

39. Righteous Businesses: Every Family was Its Own Business in the Ancient World

40. Social Justice Organizations: Prevention, Recovery, Justice, and Development

THE SEVEN SPIRITUAL DOORWAYS

WHEN MOST PEOPLE THINK ABOUT ACCESSING THE SPIRITUAL UNIVERSE, they usually think of reaching up and connecting with God. What we find is the love, joy, peace, and energy to be patient and better than we would be on our own. But God is not the only part of the spiritual universe that can be accessed. There is also a much darker and evil part of the spiritual world that can be drawn into people's lives. Connection with this darker spiritual energy can cause people to become more selfish than they would normally be, more destructive, more oppressive, and full of damaging desire. It is these access points to the darker side of the spiritual world, these *doorways*, if you will, that I want to talk about in this study. Your family may have opened some of these access points, others by your cultural heritage, or even your choices. The goal is to close these darker doorways of the spiritual universe, restricting our access only to a connection with God the Father, God the Son, and God the Holy Spirit.

A Picture of the Spiritual Universe

Imagine you are in a large heated room with seven doors. Each doorway has access to the frigid, outside air and marked with a sign that says "Do Not Open!" It is 72 degrees inside the room, but -15 degrees outside, so you do not want the outside coming in. This is a picture of spiritual warfare.

As Christians, we are living in the warm and comfortable environs of the physical universe. Around us, there is a spiritual universe that has both good and evil in it. It is very foreign to us but very real and present. (2 Kings 2:11,12; 6:15-17) When we pray, confess our sins, worship God (or practice any of the spiritual disciplines toward the one true God), we access the good and righteous parts of that spiritual universe. But when we repeatedly sin in certain ways, we open up a doorway to the evil aspects of that spiritual universe. (Eph 4:26,27) This allows a bitter, evil, and toxic influence into your life that you might not be able to see, but you feel its destructive presence.

What are these doorways that allow evil supernatural influences into people's lives? They have been called the Demonic Sins—those actions, attitudes, and/or motives that come sponsored and energized by a corrupted spiritual source. These sins will strengthen you to win at another's expense, to be destructive to your relationships, and to feel powerful as others feel weaker. In some cases, your parents or grandparents have opened these doors and have taught your family to use these sinful methods to get your way. The seven doorways we will study in this guide are:

- pride
- rebellion
- bitterness
- lust
- anger
- occult practices
- transference or generational sin

In the first study guide, *The Spiritual Disciplines*, we learned that we can access the presence of God through the spiritual disciplines because of Jesus Christ's death, resurrection, and ascension. Likewise, people can access the power of the Devil to do evil, harm, and damage through the demonic sins or evil spiritual practices. They take our natural selfishness and increase its destructive power with spiritual help. You could even call these practices, "How to be Possessed or Oppressed by the Devil."

What are the ways that we open spiritual doorways for attack, temptation, and even oppression? For thousands of years, certain activities and thoughts have been known to bring about greater spiritual, mental, and emotional bondage than others. These choices, actions, and behavioral patterns need to be brought out into the light so that we can be released from any mental, emotional, or spiritual confinement we may have been led into. Yes, these activities can be energizing, but they bring a destructive energy, not a constructive energy.

Some people, who are drunk on selfish energy, push ever deeper into these activities and pay a dreadful price for their lust for selfish power. They access spiritual doorways that strengthen themselves, but cause damage to others. Let's further define each of the seven doorways so provide a common understanding:

- **Pride:** Self-focused and self-absorbed to the detriment of others. (Isa 14:12-14)
- **Rebellion:** Pushing away righteous authority and demanding to be in charge. (1 Sam 15:23)
- **Bitterness:** Refusing to let a wound, hurt, or injustice go. (Matt 6:12, 14-15)
- **Lust:** Any excessive desire that overwhelms normal life or masks the ups and down of real life. These often include sex, drugs, food, alcohol, and the like, which allow us to cover over wounds, relationships, and hurt. (Matt 5:27-30; 1 Cor 6:12)
- **Anger:** A forceful expression of your selfish desires or unrealistic expectations. (Eph. 4:22-27)
- **Occult Practices:** Inviting spiritual entities to give you power or practicing spiritual rituals to gain advantages over others. (Deut 18:10-14; 2 Kings 21:6; Ex 20:3; Mark 12:29-31)
- **Transference:** Cursing your progeny with training in evil behavior or directly asking spirits to plague your family. (Ex 34:7b)

Repeated involvement in these areas keeps a steady influence of destructive selfishness flowing into a person's life. Usually these behavioral patterns also exert negative spiritual influences that push you further into destructive places that you never meant to go. Whatever energy they give brings a heavy price on the backside. These spiritual doorways need to be closed in your life.

Basic Elements in the Spiritual World

We were made to construct healthy, loving relationships out of the spiritual elements that God has given us. A spiritual periodic table of basic elements in the spiritual world includes: love, joy, peace, patience, kindness, goodness, gentleness, faithfulness, self-control, humility, gratefulness, curiosity, dependence, responsibility, grieving, righteous desire, mercy, grace, purity of thought, savoring life, harmony, and boundaries (personal, familial, national). Love is the basic spiritual element of the spiritual world (like hydrogen in the physical world). This is why Jesus said the two greatest commandments are, "Love God with all your heart, soul, mind, and strength," and "Love your neighbor as yourself." (Matt 22:37–40) So we must learn to construct healthy, loving relationships with God, with others, and with ourselves. *This is the point of being alive!* However, realize that what was designed for the construction of a healthy, loving relationship can be twisted and perverted for use as a selfish weapon. Pride, anger, lust, occult practices, bitterness, rebellion, and the like, open spiritual doorways to greater evil choices and influences.

Life Is Relationships

Relationships are the "construction projects" of the spiritual world and are by far the most difficult constructs to create and maintain. They require a selflessness to keep them going in a healthy way. Every time I use one of these spiritual elements selflessly, I build something constructive in the world. But if I twist love into a selfish pursuit to get what I want, then I destroy relationships and even my own soul in the process. If we are going to have the energy, the love, the joy, and the faithfulness to keep a relationship going, we must access God and His positive spiritual energy. It is our temptations, our sub-cultural messages, and evil supernaturalism that tells us that life is about possessions, power, and getting our own way. If you get your own way and all the power and all the prestige, but no one loves you, then you have gained nothing.

You Have a Choice to Make

Believe it or not, we can choose which spiritual forces to access—those that lead to blessings, or those that direct us to a wasteland. God the Father, God the Son, and God the Holy Spirit are on one side trying to direct us to His good plan for our lives—one full of blessing, purpose, adventure, and meaningful relationships. The World, the Flesh, and the Devil are on the other side trying to hide God's best from us by persuading us to make sinful choices, which are their primary weapon for our destruction. Their sole desire is to get us to miss what God wants for our life by trying to influence us, tempt us, and even trick us into wasting our lives. If they can persuade us to lean our ladder against the wrong wall or invest in the wrong things, they've gained spiritual ground. These enemies will deliver their destructive weapons of sinful choices through thoughts, emotions, and opportunities or temptations. Sinful choices are often not just isolated incidents where you have disappointed God or missed His best. They tend to be repeated areas that pull us to evil and drag us away from the good thing, causing us to miss God's blessed choice. Eventually, a spiritual doorway opens to new levels of temptation, evil influence, or destructive activity. We are told in the Scriptures that if we repeatedly give into the temptations that move us into these negative directions, then we will at some point give the Devil a place—or foothold—in our life. (Eph 4:26, 27) That is when direct interaction with evil supernaturalism takes place. (1 Sam 15:23; Deut 18:10)

God does have a great plan for our lives (Jn 10:10), but we must be active in choosing His plan, and we must use the gifts, blessings, and benefits that He has given us. Remember, you must make a choice to either follow God or choose a life of sin. If we are going to win at this spiritual war, we have to close these evil spiritual doorways so that we are free to follow God's direction.

Closing Spiritual Doorways

Throughout your Christian life, God will be working on, in, and with us. (Phil 1:6; 2:12-15) It will require work on your part to move into the freedom that is already yours in Christ Jesus. This study guide in the Weapons of Righteousness Series is designed to give you at least one exercise in each area to begin closing the spiritual doorway to evil influences. You may find that you need to go deeper in a particular area. If so, these can be explored in my book, *Becoming Courageous.* As you work through the assignments, you will learn how to close dark spiritual doorways by peeling off layers of negative emotional, mental, and spiritual influences from your life. By doing so, you will be able to lessen or close off those influences that cause you to want to win at another's expense; I think you will see that your ability to love God, others, and even yourself righteously will increase. A suggested prayer will be given for each area. This should be prayed out loud after you have spent time agreeing with God about that particular area of sinful choices. Because we will be dealing with areas of sin that could connect to strong spiritual, emotional, and/or mental influences, it is best to begin and end every session with a prayer of protection and declaration of commitment to the Lord Jesus Christ. This prayer should include a complete surrender to Jesus, an acknowledgment of Christ's complete payment for our sins on the cross, the Holy Spirit's ongoing work in our lives, and our future place in heaven. It should ask for a complete block on the Devil's power and presence, and it should turn the complete direction of this time over to the Lord Jesus Christ. The following is a sample prayer of this sort:

> ***Dear Heavenly Father,***
>
> *I come in the name of the Lord Jesus Christ and ask for your protection and direction in this time. I surrender myself to the Lord Jesus Christ and acknowledge His complete payment for my sins on the cross. I yield to the Holy Spirit's ongoing work in my life. I am excited to know that God has a wonderful plan for my life, full of good works and joy (Eph 2:10). I am thrilled that I have a future place in heaven reserved for me because of Christ's death on my behalf. I ask you, Lord Jesus, for a complete block on the Devil's presence and power in this place and with me. I ask you, Lord Jesus, to direct and protect me during my time on these exercises.*

I worship you, God, for you are all-powerful, all-knowing, present-everywhere, and unchanging. I worship you, Heavenly Father, who sent His Son, the Lord Jesus Christ, to be our Savior and Lord. I exalt you, God, because I realize you are Sovereign, True, Good, Gracious, Merciful, Loving, and Just. I am in awe of your work in Creation, Salvation, and the Scriptures. I look forward to becoming more like Christ as I cooperate with you in these exercises.

In the Name of the Lord Jesus Christ, Amen

The work you do in this study will help you discover areas where your present routines are inadequate in keeping you free from harassing thoughts, overwhelming emotions, and evil opportunities. You will also learn some new exercises and routines to help you construct healthier relationships. I do have to warn you that not everyone around you wants you to be healthier. Some of the people currently in your life have gotten used to your old way of acting and behaving, and this will be too different for them at first. Some people may want you to continue to act in unhealthy and selfish ways so that they can justify their own unhealthy and selfish behaviors. But I urge you to keep pressing forward, keep cleaning, and keep constructing your relationships in a healthy, loving way. Let's get to work and move on to the first exercise about closing the doorway of pride.

CLOSING THE DOORWAY OF PRIDE

EXERCISE #1

OVERCOMING PRIDE AND MOVING TO A PLACE OF HUMILITY

Isaiah 14:12–14

PRIDE CAN BE EITHER HEALTHY OR DESTRUCTIVE. THERE IS A HEALTHY SENSE OF personal pride in doing a job well, of keeping oneself healthy and looking sharp, or accepting congratulations for our contribution. A healthy personal pride emits a small ego field that helps us keep proper balances between rest, work, worship, relationships, recreation, purpose and the like.

The destructive form of pride is an unhealthy self-focus that destroys our future. This negative sense of pride wants to set a constant focus on oneself. It asks questions like, "Am I getting noticed enough?" "Are the right people paying attention to me?" "Is my pay or rewards as much as other people?" "Am I happy?" "Do I like the way this is turning out?" Unhealthy pride causes us to emit a growing ego field of "It's-all-about-me" energy. For some, it is a very extroverted, loud ego field. For others, it is a melancholy, hypochondriac, woe-is-me ego field. This excessive self-focus is designed to get our way. Others can sense it and feel it when they bump into it.

We are often unaware of the damage that pride does. The destructiveness of pride is the future that it takes away. Yes, accessing the spiritual energy of excessive self-focus allows you to get your own way, but it will always damage relationships and opportunities as we use this dark, spiritual energy. This is why Jesus and the apostles always counsel humility as the way to access positive spiritual energy. People will hold us back if they suspect too much of the "It's-all-about-me" energy coming from you. All of us constantly have opportunities that could open new relationships, new business endeavors, new learning arenas, and the like. But if we have a huge ego field of "It's-all-about-me" energy, this eliminates that positive future. We think we are helping people understand how great we are, but we are being self-focused and driving people away. If your relationships keep falling apart or going cold, it may be because you are accessing an excessive amount of "It's-all-about-me" energy.

Let me inject a bit of balance here so no one is led to the opposite extreme. It is not good to become a doormat for others' ideas and pride. We have to maintain a healthy personal boundary and sense of self and not lose ourselves in loving others or always giving in to others' ideas or points of view. Many times, you do have significant things to contribute and you may have to stand up for yourself in the face of another's ego field. When dealing with pride in yourself, you do not become a nothing. You become a healthy person who does not have an excessive amount of self-focus.

The Bible tells us that this was the Devil's great sin. (Ezek 28, Isa 14:12) He was the anointed cherub who functioned as the leader of all the angels. Even though he was exalted above all the other angels, he came to the place where he did not think there was enough focus on him. The other angels marveled at the wonder of God's creation in him, yet he wanted more and corrupted the normal amount of self-focus that came to him. He wanted to be like God, having others focus on him like they were focusing on God. This excessive self-focus led him to introduce sin to the universe. He now seeks to seduce all of us with the idea that a little more self-focus will fix everything. It won't; it will only corrupt us more. Pride does not grow unless there are times of unhealthy self-focus. The Devil's pride destroyed his future in God's plan and twisted his legacy into one of destruction and imprisonment.

I recently was dealing with a former pastor who was extremely gifted as a preacher and a leader. He, however, did not think that the Christian community recognized his gifts sufficiently. His growing preoccupation with how he was not being recognized or used to the full extent of his gifting and ability, caused him to eventually cut corners to become "known." It all became about him and whether he was happy. He eventually chose to begin an affair with a woman who understood how "important" he was and continually stroked his ego. He spent too much time drinking at the well of pride, and it destroyed his usefulness for the program of God.

When we are consumed in self-focus, then we are being proud and we severely damage our future. There are two directions that a self-focused "It's-all-about-me" energy can go. One direction says, "Aren't I wonderful? Everybody should focus on me." It can also say, "I have had a lot of difficult things happen to me and you should all focus on me." This thinking is still an unhealthy self-focus. Yes, there is a place for self-examination, self-reflection, and self-congratulations; but lengthy self-focus begins to rot our souls if we stay there too long. I have watched marriages crumble because of a melancholy, complaining spouse, who never has enough people agree that they have had a very tough life up to that point. Accessing this dark spiritual energy strengthens your negative outlook of the world and the bitterness at what has happened to you. It is still pride. It is still a negative self-focus, and it will destroy your relationships and your joy, even as you win the focus you think you want.

In every case, a positive relationship requires that we be others-focused. We must get outside of ourselves. Romans 12:3 tells us that we should think soberly and realistically about ourselves, neither too lofty, nor too lowly. When someone you know is always bragging, are you drawn to them or repulsed by them? When someone is always whining and complaining about themselves, their illnesses, their family, their relationships, their work, are you drawn to them? Probably not. Pride destroys these people's future because the relationships and other opportunities they could have had are never fully realized. People tend to move away from them because of their unhealthy self-focus.

Humility means realizing that we have been given abilities, gifts, and passions that need to be used for God and others. He has asked each of his servants to walk in humility with an awareness of who we are and to be open to using them for his purposes. (Matt 22:37–39; 1 Cor 12) When we truly embrace who we are and develop ourselves maximally for the glory of God and others' benefit, we will have a great life. We will be honored and rewarded for using our skills, talents, and gifts for others. (Prov 22:6; 31:28)

Pride is thinking that our talents, gifts, and passions are for us to admire or consume on ourselves. It is all about us and what we want and like. A power drill was not made to look pretty or rev the motor; it was made to drill holes. A power saw was not made to look shiny or make the blade spin fast; it was made to cut boards. Pride wants to make us look pretty and focus attention on ourselves to an inordinate degree, rather than actually honoring God and helping others. There is a place for looking our best and allowing oneself to be congratulated, but if that is what you live for, you are full of pride. Pride is like the teenagers, who fix up their cars and drive them to the High School parking lot. They show off the paint jobs and loudly rev their engines, but they never go anywhere or help anyone. God did not give us our abilities for ourselves; instead, they are meant to accomplish something for God and others.

Let's examine the ways where an unhealthy self-focus has spread through our lives and replace it with true humility. There are three parts to this exercise:

1. **Ask yourself these questions:**
   - Have I missed an opportunity to do something really good because I was too focused on myself and what I liked?

- Have I been angry because people didn't notice me enough?
- Have I not done something really good because I was afraid it would make me look bad?
- Have I ever thought I was superior to another person, thinking they are beneath me to help them?
- Have I belittled others because I could?

If you answered "yes" to any of these, there is evidence of an unhealthy self-focus in your life. Work through the next exercise and allow God to show you the ways that pride is robbing you of a much better life.

2. Uncovering Types of Pride

The following is a list of the ideas connected to pride, along with their definition. Look at each of these words and write down any times you acted towards specific people in these ways. One of the most helpful ways to proceed with this exercise is to look at the word and its definition and then prayerfully ask God if there have been any times you did this to someone. Let God bring to mind the people and the occasions where this has occurred. If He brings some incident or some person to mind, then agree with God that it was wrong and ask that your pride in that area be covered under the death of Christ. Then thank Him that it has. Also, if you are a perfectionist by nature, do not beat yourself up. This exercise is meant for cleansing, not to create new wounds or stress. Don't try and invent sins. Move on to the next word if God doesn't bring anything to your mind.

- **Pride:** Inordinate self-esteem beyond one's achievements and merit; an unhealthy self-focus

- **Arrogance:** Overbearing attitude of superiority
- **Bigotry:** Devotion to one's own opinions and prejudices without facts or before knowing the facts
- **Bragging:** Inflated or false statements about one's possessions, relationships, or achievements
- **Prejudice:** Preconceived opinion about a person or group before facts have been assessed
- **Criticism:** Act of commenting unfavorably upon the work, life, person, or behavior of others
- **Haughty:** Openly and disdainfully self-focused, bragging beyond the accomplishment's worth
- **Un-teachable:** Unwillingness to be taught; a negative reaction to learning from certain people
- **Superiority:** Exalted mental perspective about one's self
- **Disgust:** Marked aversion and repulsion to specific people or groups
- **Hypochondria:** Extreme depression of mind or soul often centered on imaginary physical ailments
- **Melancholy:** Depressive state of self-focus and irascibility
- **Depressive pride:** Fixated focus on one's problems, difficulties, obstacles, and fears
- **Self-loathing pride:** Fixation on mistakes, sins, problems, brokenness, or victimization

3. Confession

This is the time to agree with God that there have been certain times of pride in your life that have been wrong. I've given you a suggested prayer of confession. You do not have to use these exact words, but these ideas of confession, repentance, renunciation, cleansing, and transfer should be present. This is not a magical formula; it is a suggested prayer. It is your sincerity and honesty before God that is important. Also, in order for a prayer of confession to be maximally effective in breaking very powerful satanic strongholds and influence, it is best if this prayer is prayed out loud with a mature Christian brother or sister who is praying with and for you.

- **Confession and Repentance (1 John 1:9; 2 Tim 2:24)**

  Lord Jesus, I agree with you, that I have been excessively self-focused and that is wrong. I turn away from it and ask that all the forgiveness in your death on Calvary be applied to my sin in this area. I realize that only in your power and energy and through your direction can I successfully turn away from this sin.

- **Renunciation (2 Cor 4:4)**

  I repudiate, reject, and renounce any ground, place, or power I gave to Satan in my life through my involvement in unhealthy pride and an excessive self-focus. I give to the Lord Jesus Christ all power over this area of my life. I willingly surrender this area to the Lord Jesus Christ and the Holy Spirit.

- **Cleansing and Expulsion (1 John 1:9; Eph 4:27)**

  I cancel any contract I may have made with Satan through my "It's-all-about-me" attitude. I ask you, Lord Jesus, to cleanse me of any and all unrighteousness (including demons and demonic strongholds) because you say in your Word that "If we confess our sins, he is faithful and just to forgive us our sins and to cleanse us of all unrighteousness." (1 John 1:9)

- **Transfer of Ownership and Infusion of the Spirit of Truth (2 Cor 10:3-5; Col 1:27, 28; Eph 5:18)**

  I right now transfer ownership of my reputation and ego field to the Lord Jesus Christ. I choose to take every thought regarding my importance captive to Christ (2 Cor 10:3-5), and allow you full lordship in this area. I ask you, Lord Jesus, that you would fill this area of my life with the Holy Spirit of truth so that I would be wise, thankful, and able to see your plan in this area in the future. Thank you, Lord Jesus, for dying on the cross for me. I choose to cooperate with you in humility so that the process you began in me when I first trusted in you can continue. (Phil 1:6) I realize that you want to display through me your character qualities. (Col 1:27, 28; Gal 2:20)

In the Name and for the Glory of the Lord Jesus Christ, Amen

Journal of the Spiritual Exercises
Overcoming Pride and Moving to Humility

1. What I actually did:

OVERCOMING PRIDE AND MOVING TO A PLACE OF HUMILITY

2. What happened when I did it?

CLOSING SPIRITUAL DOORWAYS

3. How will I use this in the future?

CLOSING THE DOORWAY OF REBELLION

EXERCISE #2

TURNING REBELLION INTO APPROPRIATE SUBMISSION

1 Samuel 15:23; 1 Peter 2:13

EVIL SUPERNATURALISM CAN COME POURING INTO OUR LIVES THROUGH REBELLION. AN access point to evil is opened whenever we stand against wisdom and push for our own way even though it will hurt others. Rebellion means refusing to adapt myself to the needs, desires, and direction of my God-given authorities. Appropriate submission means to willingly adapt myself to the needs, desires, and commands of God-given authority without losing my dignity or personhood.

There are five major blessings or benefits that God provides when we develop the quality of appropriate submission. Developing the ability to adapt leads to protection, provision, direction, refinement, and the ability to appeal. God has placed authorities in our lives to bless us in those five specific ways. These God-given authorities are parents (until we are grown), government officials, church leaders, employers, spouses, and God Himself. They are not necessarily perfect but are in place to channel aspects of God's grace and blessing to us. When we rebel from these authorities needlessly, we miss God's best for us.

Yes, there are legitimate times to rebel from authority. Those times may come when we must submit to a higher authority than a particular authority. If one of our authorities is forcing us to violate God's laws, then we must courageously submit to God's higher laws and resist the unethical authority. (Dan 3; 6)

When people are unwilling to take direction from authority, they are also unable to take direction from God. Rebellion often leaves people vulnerable to greater temptation and robs them of being in the center of God's will. (1 Sam 15:23) These exercises will help you develop a healthy relationship with authority. There are many more exercises in the book *Becoming Courageous* that can further develop a healthy interaction with authority.

1. **If we were to ask your God-given authorities about how you deal with them, would they say you adapt to their leadership, or are you stubborn, hard to work with, and even rebellious?**

Parents:

Government officials:

Employers:

Spouse:

Church leaders:

God:

2. Confession

This is the time to agree with God that certain times of rebellion in your life have been wrong. There is not a magical formula, but I've given you a suggested prayer of confession. You do not have to use these exact words, but these ideas of confession, repentance, renunciation, cleansing, and transfer should be present. It is your sincerity and honesty before God that is important. Also, in order for a prayer of confession to be maximally effective in breaking very powerful satanic strongholds and influence, it is best if this prayer is prayed out loud with a mature Christian brother or sister praying with and for you.

- **Confession and Repentance (1 John 1:9; 2 Tim 2:24)**

    Lord Jesus, I agree with you that rebellion is wrong. I turn away from it and ask that all the forgiveness that is in your death on Calvary be applied to my sin in this area. You say in your Word that rebellion is like the sin of witchcraft. I realize that only in your power, energy, and through your direction can I successfully turn away from this sin.

- **Renunciation (2 Cor 4:4)**

    I repudiate, reject, and renounce any ground, place, or power I gave to Satan in my life through my involvement in rebellion. I give to the Lord Jesus Christ all power over this area of my life. I willingly surrender this area to the Lord Jesus Christ and the Holy Spirit.

- **Cleansing and Expulsion (1 John 1:9; Eph 4:27)**

    I cancel any contract I may have made with Satan through rebellion. I ask you, Lord Jesus, to cleanse me of any and all unrighteousness (including demons and demonic strongholds), because you say in your Word that "if we confess our sins, He is faithful and just to forgive us our sins and to cleanse us of all unrighteousness." (1 John 1:9)

- **Transfer of Ownership and Infusion of the Spirit of Truth (2 Cor 10:3–5; Col 1:27, 28; Eph 5:18)**

    I, right now, transfer ownership of adaptation and followership to the Lord Jesus Christ. I choose to take every thought regarding rebellion captive to Christ (2 Cor 10:3–5) and allow Him full lordship in this area. I ask you, Lord Jesus, that you would fill this area of my life with the Holy Spirit of truth so that I would be wise, thankful, and able to see your plan in this area in the future. Thank you, Lord Jesus, for dying on the cross for me. I choose to cooperate with you in being a team player so that the process you began in me when I first trusted in you can continue. (Phil 1:6) I realize that you want to display through me your character qualities. (Col 1:27, 28; Gal 2:20)

    In the Name and for the Glory of the Lord Jesus Christ, Amen

3. Ask yourself, "If I were to adapt myself to my God-given authorities (while not sacrificing my dignity or personhood), what five things would be different in my life?"

   1.

   2.

   3.

   4.

   5.

If you don't know, then ask your authority how you could change to line up with their needs. You might be surprised by what they say.

Journal of the Spiritual Exercises Turning Rebellion into Appropriate Submission

1. What I actually did:

TURNING REBELLION INTO APPROPRIATE SUBMISSION

2. What happened when I did it?

3. How will I use this in the future?

CLOSING THE DOORWAY OF BITTERNESS

EXERCISE #3

TURNING BITTERNESS INTO A FORGIVING HEART

Matthew 6:12, 14–15; 18:21–35

Evil supernaturalism also comes pouring in through bitterness. Whenever there are demonic forces at work, you will always find bitterness—that is, anger, resentment, and disappointment for unfair treatment or unmet expectations. The goal of forgiveness is to be free from the damaging impact of the past. We may always carry the scars of the past, but we do not have to be imprisoned by them. Many people underestimate the need for forgiveness. Without forgiveness, we are not pursuing our mission in life; we are trying to pay back the injustice of others. Many allow bitterness to become their reason for living, refusing to let go of the offenses of others instead of finding their true purpose and unique, positive contribution.

God never designed us to carry around bitterness. He tells us many times throughout the Bible that we are to rid ourselves of all poison-producing bitterness because it keeps us captive to sin and defiles our lives and relationships with others. (Deut 29:18; Acts 8:23; Eph 4:31; Heb 12:15) Instead, He commands us to forgive. Why? Because there is healing in forgiveness. The joy of forgiveness enables us to move on with our lives and not allow the evil or hurt caused by others to keep haunting us. He also commands us to let Him handle the justice piece—as long as we keep trying to hold a person responsible for the wrong they did to us, God and the proper authorities will not be free to work. (Rom 12:19) Forgiveness is a conscious choice, beginning with the desire to be free from the weight of personally executing justice.

To begin the process of healing, forgiveness can take place through a very complex process involving many different exercises. I've given you one exercise in this study guide that will help begin the process of that healing. Many more exercises and essential work in forgiveness are included in the book, *Becoming Courageous*.

Forgiveness involves three basic areas:
1. Developing a forgiving heart that is able to let the offense go;

2. Making sure that your conscience is clear in regard to this offense;

3. Embracing the lessons and training that can come from this offense.

While the exercise below may seem impossible, it causes you to apply the principles of forgiveness found in the New Testament. This process will take time and will move you to think in new ways; however, being free from the enslaving attitudes of bitterness is worth it. Think of this time as being in a cocoon while you become a completely transformed person, able to forgive people and not letting their selfishness derail your future.

Step 1: Write out a list of those who have deeply wounded you, what they did, and how often. Also think through whether you had any part in causing or increasing what they did to you.

Most people do not have more than twenty people who have deeply wronged them; but if you do, keep writing and noting what they did. We may have hundreds of people who have been rude, offensive, irritating, or bothersome, but we usually have few who really have wounded us or wronged us deeply. Even as you read this there are a few people who probably come to mind. It is those deep wounds that we are going after in this exercise. Some people may have hurt us in a number of different ways at a number of different times. I would suggest that you write using initials or in some code that only you will know, so that these painful memories stay private until you are ready to reveal them. We have provided this list of offenses in Step 2 below.

CLOSING SPIRITUAL DOORWAYS

Who has deeply hurt you?

Name/Initials	What they did:	How often:	Your part:
1.			
2.			
3.			
4.			
5.			
6.			
7.			

Step 2: Determine whether what they did was wrong or just offensive.

In the process of letting go of bitterness, it is important to label the nature of the offense. All societies have different levels of improper activities. These range from the criminal, to the socially offensive. Let's spend some time looking at types of offenses so we can label them more accurately. These are general categories and the definitions are decidedly broad.

- **Criminal Offense:** This is where a person is harming others in some way and will most likely continue to harm others if they are not stopped. This would be like murder, rape, stealing, armed robbery, or extortion.

- **Civil Offense:** This is where the person has harmed another person in some way, but they may not continue doing it to others. This might be where one neighbor damaged their neighbor's fence, car, or dog for some reason.

- **Organizational Offense:** This is where a person has offended, harmed, or hurt another person, but their actions were a part of an organizational policy, order, or decision. This might be where a person is fired, reprimanded, or reassigned by their employer.

- **Unethical Offense:** This is an offense that is not technically or legally wrong but is clearly selfish, wounding, or put the offended in a bad position. This might be where a person lies about their age on a form to get a leg up for a promotion, or where a person uses their friendship with another person to push them ahead of a more qualified applicant for a promotion.

- **Accidental Offense:** This is one in which the offender did not mean to do the action or did not understand that the action would result in what took place. This might be where a person did not know the brakes on the car were bad, or they did not intend to lose control of the car as they sped out of the parking lot; or they did not understand the power of the rifle or that it was loaded.

- **Familial Offense:** This is a wound, hurt, or offense that takes place in a family or in a family's culture. This might be where a pet name used in a family becomes offensive to someone as they grow up. It may also be that a family ritual becomes offensive.

- **Religious Offense:** This is an offense where the particular rituals, restrictions, or understandings of a religion are violated or a person was made to violate them. This may be where a person is made to listen to blasphemies about their faith practices. It may be where a person is made to participate or watch what is forbidden by their religion.

- **Personal Offense:** This is an offense that is personally offensive or harmful but not organizationally, civically, or criminally liable. This may be a name or action that is used. It could be almost any action that another person continues to do after you have asked them to stop.

- **Everyday Offense:** This is an offense, hurt, or wound that regularly takes place but does not rise to ethical or legal standards of wrong. This might be a slight, a word, an action, or an attitude that demeans you or marginalizes you from your point of view. Sometimes we are wounded or offended by another's actions, but their actions were not wrong. They just irritated us or were offensive in some other personal way. However, if their offenses were criminally wrong or morally wrong, then we are to declare them as wrong.

Many people can never forgive or forget because they cannot label an offense as wrong. It might be because it is a loved one who committed it or because they feel responsible for the person. We must be willing to label an offense correctly. "That was morally wrong!" "That was offensive!" "That was just irritating!" "That was criminal!" Take each offense from the previous list and put it in a category below. Use the categories listed below to categorize the offense on a rough scale of evil. Let's take a look at the offenses in your life in more detail.

CLOSING SPIRITUAL DOORWAYS

Label the offense:

	Name/Initials	Category of Offense	Wrong or just offensive?
1.			
2.			
3.			
4.			
5.			
6.			
7.			

Step 3: Choose to Forgive. Forgiveness at its core is a choice to no longer be the one who wants to mete out punishment, justice, or fairness to the person.

God tells us to hand that over to Him. They have done what they have done and you must move past it. There is a life to live and new choices to make. You cannot allow the choice they made go on affecting the choices you need to make. Pray a prayer like this:

Dear Heavenly Father;

"I come to you in the name of the Lord Jesus Christ, who died on my behalf that I could be forgiven of all my sins. I choose to turn _____ (name the person) over to you God for any punishment, justice, or blessing they deserve. (Rom 12:31) You know where they are. You know what needs to be done more than I do. You have told me that I cannot handle carrying the need for vengeance or bitterness, so I hand it over to you so that you can give them what they deserve. I would like to make the following suggestions to you as to what they deserve...

1. _____

2. _____

3. _____

4. _____

5. _____

> *I am giving all vengeance and bitterness over to you, so that I can move on with my life and not have their memory or their actions in any way controlling my own. I realize that only as I pursue loving you, God, and the other people that you have placed in my life, will I have the kind of life I really desire. Getting revenge or even justice on another person will not satisfy me. I want a blessed life that comes from love, grace, mercy, forgiveness, and a positive outlook."*

There are many ways to choose to forgive, but ultimately it becomes a choice to let God handle it and move on with your life. Yes, what they did may have been deeply evil and hurtful, but it is in the past, and you need to move into the future.

Journal of the Spiritual Exercises
Turning Bitterness into a Forgiving Heart

1. What I actually did:

CLOSING SPIRITUAL DOORWAYS

2. What happened when I did it?

3. **How will I use this in the future?**

CLOSING THE DOORWAY OF LUST

EXERCISE #4

OVERCOMING LUST AND DEVELOPING A PURE HEART

*Matthew 5:38; 2 Timothy 2:22;
1 Corinthians 6:18, 19*

THERE IS AMAZING JOY AND LIBERATION IN PURITY. PURITY IS ABOUT THINKING, speaking, and acting in a pure, wholesome, or uncontaminated manner. It is being truly beneficial to yourself, others, and society. Purity is not always what we want, but it is what we need. Deep inside we crave purity and the life-giving energy it gives. There is great joy and peace in being pure.

Think about eating pure, life-giving, healthy food. Think about breathing pure, life-giving, healthy air. Think about drinking pure, life-giving, healthy water. Purity gives life. Purity brings health. Purity reenergizes and restores. Too often in Christian circles we think of purity in terms of what it is not. This approach can cause us to fixate on what we don't want to do, say, or think. But sometimes that causes us to focus on the impure. Purity is about the joy, health, and peace of positive personal and relational behavior.

There are hundreds of things that are damaging, destructive, and poisonous and need to be eliminated, but we must be focused on purity. To pursue purity is to go after the actions, thoughts, or words that will be the most beneficial to oneself and to others. Becoming pure is not about saying "no" as much as it is about saying "yes" to healthy relationships, "yes" to life-giving thoughts, "yes" to deep intimacy with God, "yes" to soul-enriching activities, and "yes" to restorative community activities. It is almost impossible to win against impurity by focusing on saying "no," but it is possible to grow more and more in purity by aiming at healthy relationships, healthy thought patterns, healthy activities, and life-giving good works. In order to be pure, you will have to say "no" to what is toxic, draining, and poisonous to your life and relationships, but the focus is not on "no."

With this understanding, it is possible to grasp what lust is. Lust is an inordinate desire for anything, anyone, or any activity that destroys health, purity, peace, and joy in your life. Lust is an inordinate desire for what is impure—for what will damage oneself, others, or society. There are hundreds of actions, thoughts, and words that seem exciting and pleasurable, but they do significant damage to us, to others, or to the society at large. This is what lust is.

Let me give you an example. There are things (pornography, affairs, strip clubs, prostitutes) that a man can pursue that will significantly damage his wife and his children. They may be very enjoyable things for him but very damaging for the family. He may not experience the damage that comes from doing them initially. In fact, he may enjoy the activity so much that he does not mind any damage that accrues to him personally. If he focuses on how much he personally enjoys doing these things, then he will always be tempted to do them even though his family will suffer. If selfishness takes over, then what he wants will always win no matter who is harmed. But if the question is, "How can everyone in my life win?" then we get a different answer. Lust is pursuing something toxic to oneself or to others. It doesn't matter how much we like it or whether we can handle it. The question is what that pursuit does to you, to the relationships of your life, and to the society at large.

Let me give you a few other examples:

- Someone may really like shopping and spending money. It helps their mood and keeps them happy. But no matter how much they enjoy it, if their family does not have the money to pay for what they need to buy, then this fun thing will destroy the family's security and stability.

- Someone may enjoy listening and spreading the problems of others. It does not matter how much they enjoy this activity, they may be damaging their relationships and others' ability to trust them.

- Someone may enjoy a hobby so much that they spend a lot of time and money on it so that family needs are left undone. The hobby has become a toxic thing. Usually when a person is pursuing some impure thing that is damaging, there is some enjoyable, pure activity that they are completely missing. At times, people feel that if they give up the destructive impure thing, there is nothing to do but be bored. This is never the case. Purity is more exciting and life-giving than impurity. It is only an illusion that impurity gives life and does not destroy. It always destroys; that is why it is called "impurity."

We all want to receive pure, encouraging, positive words, thoughts, and actions from others because these are so life-giving. There is purity all around us. We just have to be trained to notice it. Impurity is screaming at us so that we will not see the purity that is so much better for us. Make no mistake; there are toxic elements in our society that will destroy the individual, marriages, families, and even the communities of the people who pursue them. The usual impure suspects are alcohol, drugs, prostitution, gambling, pornography, and the like.

Jesus does not want us to be focused on saying "no" to lust, but instead to say "yes" to purity. (Matt 5:6; 8) It is purity that heals. It is purity that brings joy. It is purity that brings stability and health. What does a pure romantic relationship look like? What does a pure positive parent-child relationship look like? What does a pure positive energetic worker look like? When you can answer what purity looks like, then you can pursue it. It is not enough to try and stay away from impurity. My wife wants me to do so much more in our marriage than stay away from affairs and pornography. She and I both want a live-giving, pure relationship of love that fills our souls and energizes our lives. Of course, that kind of relationship avoids affairs and pornography.

Temptation is always a distraction and it is always a form of selfishness. When God is about to present His options for you, then the World, the Flesh, and the Devil will present some temptation that makes going after the Lord's perfect plan for you less attractive and easy. What forms of excessive desires tempt you and move you away from God's best?

- Food
- Clothing
- Sex
- Alcohol
- Drugs
- Power
- Fame (popularity)
- Money

Confessing your sins of excessive desire. (1 John 1:9; Matt 5:11)

We absolutely have to get a handle on where our excessive desire for certain things will derail God's best for our life. Pray the prayer of confession over each of the times you have sinned in these ways. There is something very powerful about admitting to God that you have been involved in significant sexual, selfish behavior. Remember that there is forgiveness in Jesus Christ. He is not waiting to condemn, but to comfort and forgive those who admit they have been destroying their own lives by going beyond God's plan for sexuality.

Take each person and situation where you have gone outside God's plan for sexuality and admit to God that you were wrong. There is not a magical formula, but I've given you a suggested prayer of confession. You do not have to use these exact words, but these ideas of confession, repentance, renunciation, cleansing, and transfer should be present. It is your sincerity and honesty before God that is important.

Also, in order for a prayer of confession to be maximally effective in breaking very powerful satanic strongholds and influence, it is best if this prayer is prayed out loud with a mature Christian brother or sister who is watching you pray and is praying with and for you.

1. **Confession and Repentance (1 John 1:9; 2 Tim 2:24)**

    Lord Jesus, I agree with you that my excessive desire for _____ is wrong. I turn away from it and ask that all the forgiveness that is in your death on Calvary be applied to my sin in this area. You say in your Word that lust in all of its forms is wrong. I realize that only in your power and through your direction can I successfully turn away from this sin.

2. **Renunciation (2 Cor 4:4)**

    I repudiate, reject, and renounce any ground, place, or power I gave to Satan in my life through my excessive desire for _____. I give to the Lord Jesus Christ all power over this area of my life. I willingly surrender this area to the Lord Jesus Christ and the Holy Spirit.

3. **Cleansing and Expulsion (1 John 1:9; Eph 4:27)**

    I cancel any contract I may have made with Satan because of my excessive desire for _____. I ask you, Lord Jesus, to cleanse me of any and all unrighteousness (including demons and demonic strongholds) because you say in your Word that "If we confess our sins, He is faithful and just to forgive us our sins and to cleanse us of all unrighteousness." (1 John 1:9)

4. **Transfer of Ownership and Infusion of the Spirit of Truth (2 Cor 10:3–5; Col. 1:27, 28; Eph 5:18)**

   I right now transfer ownership of my desire to the Lord Jesus Christ. I choose to take every thought regarding _____ (the area where lust tempts you) captive to Christ (2 Cor 10:3-5) and allow Him full lordship in this area. I ask you, Lord Jesus, that you would fill this area of my life with the Holy Spirit of truth, so that I would be wise, thankful, and able to see your plan in this area in the future. Thank you, Lord Jesus, for dying on the cross for me. I choose to cooperate with you in my interaction with _____ so that the process you began in me when I first trusted in you can continue. (Phil 1:6) I realize that you want to display through me your character qualities. (Col 1:27, 28; Gal 2:20)

   In the Name and for the Glory of the Lord Jesus Christ, Amen

Journal of the Spiritual Exercises Overcoming Lust and Developing a Pure Heart

1. What I actually did:

2. **What happened when I did it?**

CLOSING SPIRITUAL DOORWAYS

3. How will I use this in the future?

EXERCISE #5

MEDITATING ON SCRIPTURE TO OVERCOME TEMPTATION

TEMPTATION IS LIKE A TOXIC WIND THAT BLOWS INTO OUR LIVES AND SEEKS TO corrupt our ability to love and do good things for others. Quoting or reading Scripture slowly and deliberately allows you to dive under the wave of temptation that has always beaten you before. Slowly repeat key Scriptures each day, especially when you are being tempted to do something to excess. Don't be in a hurry to say the verse; slowly speak it almost as an answer to the temptation you are facing. You may even feel the power of the temptation pass over you as you continue to slowly repeat the Scriptures. This action of repeating Scriptures slowly and deliberately pushes back against the corrupting power of the temptation. You will be surprised at how powerful these verses make you in your battle against temptation.

Years ago, my youth pastor made me memorize each of the verses provided in this exercise. I was asked to produce ten pages of biblical meditation on each verse and then he asked me to live them out whenever I faced temptation. This assignment changed my life. I had new-found power from the life of God in the Scriptures that allowed me to resist the destructive temptations that could have so easily ripped my life apart. I cannot recommend this exercise highly enough.

In doing this exercise, you might want to write each verse on a card to carry with you and slowly read it over and over (out loud) as you are facing a temptation. You may find that some verses work better for you than other verses against specific temptations.

- 1 Corinthians 3:13—*"Each man's work will become evident; for the day will show it because it is to be revealed with fire, and the fire itself will test the quality of each man's work."*

- 2 Corinthians 10:3-5—*"For though we walk in the flesh, we do not war according to the flesh, for the weapons of our warfare are not of the flesh, but divinely powerful for the destruction of fortresses. We are destroying speculations and every lofty thing raised up against the knowledge of God, and we are taking every thought captive to the obedience of Christ."*

- James 1:2-4—*"Consider it all joy, my brethren, when you encounter various trials, knowing that the testing of your faith produces endurance. And let endurance have its perfect result, so that you may be perfect and complete, lacking in nothing."*

- 1 Thessalonians 4:3-5—*"For this is the will of God, your sanctification; that is, that you abstain from sexual immorality; that each of you know* how to possess his own vessel in sanctification and honor, not in lustful passion, like the Gentiles who do not know God."

- Romans 6:11-13—"*Even so, consider yourselves dead to sin but alive to God in Christ Jesus. Therefore, do not let sin reign in your mortal body so that you obey its lusts, and do not go on presenting the members of your body to sin as instruments of unrighteousness; but present yourselves to God as those alive from the dead, and your members as instruments of righteousness to God.*"

- Galatians 5:16—"*But I say, walk by the Spirit, and you will not carry out the desire of the flesh.*"

- Galatians 5:22, 23—"*But the fruit of the Spirit is love, joy, peace, patience, kindness, goodness, faithfulness, gentleness, self-control; against such things there is no law.*"

- Galatians 5:24—"*Now those who belong to Christ Jesus have crucified the flesh with its passions and desires.*"

- Colossians 3:2, 5—"*Set your mind on the things above, not on the things that are on earth. Therefore, consider the members of your earthly body as dead to immorality, impurity, passion, evil desire, and greed, which amounts to idolatry.*"

- Hebrews 12:11, 12—"*All discipline for the moment seems not to be joyful, but sorrowful; yet to those who have been trained by it, afterwards it yields the peaceful fruit of righteousness. Therefore, strengthen the hands that are weak and the knees that are feeble."

- Psalm 1:1-3—"How blessed is the man who does not walk in the counsel of the wicked, nor stand in the path of sinners, nor sit in the seat of scoffers! But his delight is in the law of the Lord, and in His law, he meditates day and night. He will be like a tree firmly planted by streams of water, which yields its fruit in its season and its leaf does not wither; and in whatever he does, he prospers."

- Proverbs 15:3—"The eyes of the Lord are in every place, watching both the evil and the good."

- Psalm 119:9,11—"How can a young man keep his way pure? By keeping it according to Your word. Your word I have treasured in my heart, That I may not sin against You."

- Judges 16:21—"Then the Philistines seized him and gouged out his eyes; and they brought him down to Gaza and bound him with bronze chains, and he was a grinder in the prison."

- Psalm 19:14—"Let the words of my mouth and the meditation of my heart be acceptable in Your sight, O Lord, my rock and my Redeemer."

- Job 31:1—"I have made a covenant with my eyes, how then could I gaze at a virgin?"

- Romans 12:1, 2—"Therefore I urge you, brethren, by the mercies of God, to present your bodies a living and holy sacrifice, acceptable to God, which is your spiritual service of worship. And do not be *conformed to this world, but be transformed by the renewing of your mind, so that you may prove what the will of God is, that which is good and acceptable and perfect."*

Journal of the Spiritual Exercises Meditating on Scripture to Overcome Temptation

1. What I actually did:

2. **What happened when I did it?**

3. How will I use this in the future?

CLOSING THE DOORWAY OF ANGER

EXERCISE #6

TURNING ANGER INTO A CONTROLLED SOUL

Ephesians 4:22–27

ANOTHER DOORWAY OF ACCESS TO EVIL SUPERNATURALISM IS THROUGH ANGER, rage, and seething resentment. Many do not see anger as a problem. In fact, many use it as a tool or a weapon to get their way. I have a friend who is wonderful except for the hand grenade of anger she carries with her. She rarely uses it, but she is always ready to throw an anger bomb. She is a wonderful mother, a wonderful wife, and an exemplar employee. She regularly gets praise for how she acts in each of these roles, going above and beyond the call of duty ninety-nine percent of the time. But after about a month or six weeks, she verbally vomits on the people in her life. She is angry and she lets the people around her have it. She's been known to hold her colleagues at work hostage to her rants. She has blown through a number of husbands, who at some point have refused to put up with this withering barrage of emotional venom. Her children tip toe around wondering if Mt. Mom is about to blow. If you ask her, she looks at the ninety-nine percent of her life that is wonderful and righteous and loving and says to herself that she is a really good person. Everyone else who has ever experienced the volcano of her anger walks with nervousness around her. She truly cannot understand why people have a problem with her; in her mind, she only occasionally gets mad. The wonderful work that she does most of the time more than makes up for her rants. But that is not how others see it. They give her a wide berth. They make excuses why she is not included in their close circle of friends. There is a reason she has not married again.

Here are three things we need to know about our relationship with anger.

1. **Anger is an emotional reaction to something in your life.** Over time, your soul has been tuned by experiences and choices of the past that cause you to react with anger to whatever just happened. Not everyone reacts in exactly the same way to what just happened, but your anger is unique. Something specific triggers the anger inside of you. Your anger is like the sound that comes from guitar strings that have been strummed. Your anger is like a rash that bubbles up when you brush up against poison oak. Your anger is an allergic rash you have developed to life when it presents itself to you in this way. Now the important thing to realize is that you can change this reaction in a number of ways. It is up to you to choose to change this reaction so you do not disqualify yourself from higher levels of love, meaning, joy, and honor. Think of three triggers that draw out

anger in you. This could be a person, a situation, a memory, specific words, an event, and so on.

1.

2.

3.

2. **You can learn to react in a different way to this anger problem.** You'll have to explore what ways you can choose to react to the situation, problem, people, or pressures in a different way other than anger. This will be an attempt to create a completely different reactive pattern here. Realize that you know people who do not react with anger to exactly the same situation that produces anger in you. What they are doing differently? How do they channel their reaction down a different path than you are channeling yours? Be very specific here. "I could do this, say this, or reward myself in this particular way if I didn't get angry." "Or, I could choose to laugh it off in this way," and so forth. Think of three ways you could react differently next time you feel the urge to get angry:

1.

2.

3.

Let me suggest a few others:
- Laughter
- Taking notes
- Push-ups
- Some form of physical movement or exercise
- Quoting Scripture—out loud or under your breath
- Psychoanalyzing the other person or yourself
- Pinching yourself
- Deep breaths
- Examining your expectations for the trigger

If you usually get angry every time you are around Jim or Sally for more than a few minutes, then what different reactions could you develop so that you will not get angry if you are around them for a while? If you usually get angry when you go to a party at a certain place or with certain people, then what different reactions could you develop so you will not get angry? If you usually get angry when you are under time or financial pressures, then what different reactions could you develop to avoid getting angry?

3. **Anger in its raw form is destructive and must be refined to be utilized.** The raw energy of anger must be refined if it is to become a constructive force in our lives. Anger in its raw form blames, criticizes, mopes, attacks, plots, schemes. You can't put raw anger into your life and expect it not to damage relationships, work, finances, future plans, and the like. The presence

TURNING ANGER INTO A CONTROLLED SOUL

of anger is a signal that change is needed in some part of your life. The Devil wants us to focus so much on our anger that we miss the real change that is needed.

Much of destructive anger is about unrealistic expectations. We expected something to happen, but it did not. Our expectations may be good, but it is unrealistic given the people and situation. There are many times when I am tempted to give in to anger and then I realize that I did not communicate clearly what I was hoping would happen. Other times I was expecting people to read my mind. Still other times there was no way for other people to meet my expectations, and therefore, they were unrealistic. We need to come to grips with the various forms of our anger in their destructive forms and understand how long anger has been a part of our lives and our family background. The Devil will often work with anger as a base of operation in a person's life. (Eph 4:26, 27)

Let's take a look at your anger. Work through this checklist of expressions of anger and pray the prayer of confession and repentance at the end.

Check	Involvement with Anger, Violence, or Murder	Do you do this? How often?
	Outbursts of anger	
	Rage	
	Wrath—seething when in that person's presence	

CLOSING SPIRITUAL DOORWAYS

Check	Involvement with Anger, Violence, or Murder	Do you do this? How often?
	Burning resentment—inability to escape thinking about what they did and what you would like to do back	
	Malice—delighting in planning harm to the person; doing harm to them	
	Violence against others—often to get your own way	
	Assault—physical, sexual, financial	
	Murder— mental/emotional, racial, abortion, physical, spiritual, sexual	

Take the time to ask God for forgiveness for your destructive anger and the way it has messed with your life and your family's life. Admit that anger is wrong. Turn over this area of change, expectations, and power to God. The following is a suggested prayer in confessing your anger.

A Prayer of Confession

Take each person and/or situation where you have demonstrated raw anger and admit to God that you were wrong. This is not a magical formula; it is a suggested prayer. But the ideas of confession, repentance, renunciation, cleansing, and transfer are powerful. It is your sincerity and honesty before God that is important. Also, in order for a prayer of confession to be maximally effective in breaking very powerful satanic strongholds and influence, it is best if this prayer is prayed out loud with a mature Christian brother or sister who is watching you pray and is praying with and for you.

1. **Confession and Repentance (1 John 1:9; 2 Tim 2:24)**

   Lord Jesus, I agree with you that anger is wrong. I turn away from it and ask that all the forgiveness that is in your death on Calvary be applied to my sin in this area. You say in your Word that anger, rage, and hatred is wrong, for you say, "The anger of man does not achieve the righteousness of God." I realize that only in your power and through your direction can I successfully turn away from this sin.

2. **Renunciation (2 Cor 4:4)**

   I repudiate, reject, and renounce any ground, place, or power I gave to Satan in my life through my involvement in anger. I give to the Lord Jesus Christ all power over this area of my life. I willingly surrender this area to the Lord Jesus Christ and the Holy Spirit.

3. **Cleansing and Expulsion (1 John 1:9; Eph 4:27)**

   I cancel any contract I may have made with Satan through anger. I ask you, Lord Jesus, to cleanse me of any and all unrighteousness (including demons and demonic strongholds) because you say in your Word that "If we confess our sins, He is faithful and just to forgive us our sins and to cleanse us of all unrighteousness." (1 John 1:9)

4. **Transfer of Ownership and Infusion of the Spirit of Truth (2 Cor 10:3-5; Col 1:27, 28; Eph 5:18)**

   I right now transfer ownership of change and expectations in my life to the Lord Jesus Christ. I choose to take every thought regarding anger, change, and expectations captive to Christ (2 Cor 10:3-5) and allow Him full lordship in this area. I ask you, Lord Jesus, to fill this area of my life with the Holy Spirit of truth, so that I would be wise, thankful, and able to see your plan in this area in the future. Thank you, Lord Jesus, for dying on the cross for me. I choose to cooperate with you in developing calm flexibility so that the process you began in me when I first trusted in you can continue. (Phil 1:6) I realize that you want to display through me your character qualities. (Col 1:27,28; Gal 2:20)

   In the Name and for the Glory of the Lord Jesus Christ, Amen

Journal of the Spiritual Exercises
Turning Anger into a Controlled Soul

1. What I actually did:

2. What happened when I did it?

3. How will I use this in the future?

CLOSING THE DOORWAY OF OCCULT PRACTICES

EXERCISE #7

TURNING OCCULT INVOLVEMENT INTO WORSHIP OF GOD ALONE

Matthew 4:4; Exodus 20:3–6

MANY PEOPLE HAVE BEEN LED ASTRAY IN THEIR LIVES BY TURNING TO THE OCCULT for spiritual meaning and strength. The occult represents the worship of other false gods and the pursuit of supernatural power for personal reasons. This is an obvious doorway to evil supernaturalism and is very dangerous. If one is going to become serious about experiencing freedom in Christ, then God's demands for exclusive worship must be taken seriously. (Ex 20:3,4) Cutting ties with other gods and beginning to worship the God of the Bible exclusively and fully is one of the most serious actions a person of faith can take. I've outlined the following steps to move one from observer of God to a true worshipper and citizen of heaven.

Step 1: Become a fully committed Christian.

The one antidote to the problems associated with past occult involvement is a complete surrender to the Lord Jesus Christ. If you have never asked Jesus Christ to save you from your sins and run your life, then ask Him right now. While the other steps to getting rid of occult bondage can be done, they are of little value without a fully surrendered life. If you are a Christian who has been backsliding or is not fully committed, then it is time to rededicate your life to God. The only barrier that the Devil respects is the blood of the Lord Jesus Christ. You must be fully dedicated to Jesus Christ—no half-hearted measures will work.

Step 2: Make the ultimate trade.

God has offered to make one of the most lopsided trades of all time. In order to appreciate the trade that He offers, we must understand heaven's requirements. There is only one way to gain entrance into heaven and that is to be absolutely perfect. (Matt 5:48; Ezek 18:4)

Let's suppose that a couple is married and the husband is absolutely perfect. When he arrives in heaven, the pearly gates swing wide open. He enjoys the benefits and blessings of heaven as the result of having lived an absolutely perfect life. Now let's also suppose that while he is in heaven, he remembers his wife back on earth. He loves her so much and wants her to be able to experience heaven, too. But he knows his wife cannot get into heaven because heaven is a perfect place and she is not perfect. He decides to go to God to propose a trade. He tells God that he will gladly trade all of his perfection for her sin and God agrees to the plan. So, the husband comes back to earth and tells his wife about this plan, this trade. He tells her about how wonderful heaven is and how much she would enjoy it; she wants that for herself, too, so she agreed to trade all of her sin and wrongdoings for his perfection. Now, when it's her time to approach the gates of heaven, they will swing wide for her, too, because she was made perfect through the sacrifice her husband made on her behalf.

The only problem is that heaven cannot be accessed based on a sacrifice or trade made by ordinary men and women. It's impossible for us to live perfect lives, so giving it up for another wouldn't work. God Himself must make the trade, since He is without sin; "He made Him who knew no sin to be sin on our behalf that we might become the righteousness of God." (2 Cor 5:21) There is still only one person in heaven—God, whose life never ends. He loves the whole world and wants heaven to be available to everyone; "The Lord is not slow in keeping his promise, as some understand slowness. Instead he is patient with you, not wanting anyone to perish, but everyone to come to repentance." (2 Pet 3:9) He became that perfect man, Jesus Christ, who lived a perfect life and then gave it up to save mankind from eternal death; "For God so loved the world that he gave his one and only Son, that whoever believes in him shall not perish but have eternal life. (John 3:16) This trade is offered to everyone—there is no limit to the number of people that can accept it. As many as are willing to trade their sins for Christ's perfection will be given entrance into heaven; "But to as many as received Him He gave them the right to be the children of God." (John 1:12) As a part of the trade, Jesus Christ becomes our Lord and Master and we are to follow him with the whole of our lives. In other words, there is to be a complete surrender to the One who was willing to take our sins; "Then Jesus said to his disciples, "Whoever wants to be my disciple must deny themselves and take up their cross and follow me." (Matt 16:24)

What about you? Have you made the ultimate trade?

You can do so now by repeating a prayer that goes something like this:

Dear Heavenly Father,

I realize that I am a sinner and not perfect enough to earn my way into heaven. I need your payment for my sins—the Lord Jesus Christ's death on the cross. I want to make the trade with Christ right now. He takes all my sin, and I receive all his perfection. I realize that when I make this trade, it means that I want Jesus Christ to run my life. I also give you permission to make me the kind of person you want me to be. I thank you, Lord Jesus, for dying on the cross for me. I do want you to trade your perfection for my sin. I will let you be the boss of my life. Thank you.

In the Name Lord Jesus, Amen

Journal of the Spiritual Exercises Turning Occult Involvements into Worship of God Alone

1. What I actually did:

2. What happened when I did it?

3. How will I use this in the future?

EXERCISE #8

RIDDING YOUR HOUSE OF OCCULT OBJECTS

THERE MAY OBJECTS IN YOUR HOME THAT CAN GIVE THE DEVIL AN ADVANTAGE IN YOUR life. They need to be rooted out and destroyed. (Deut 18:9-11) The scriptural method for destroying these objects is by smashing and/or burning (Ex 32:19,20; Judg 6:25-28). This renders the objects unusable, and therefore, unwanted by another. It is recommended to pray after the objects have been destroyed and state the command: "Satan and the demons are no longer welcome here and must leave in the name of the Lord Jesus Christ. Whatever ground or place may have been given to Satan through my possession or use of this object is canceled and given completely over to the Lord Jesus Christ to be occupied by the Holy Spirit."

Following is a suggested list of items that may be in your home:

Occult Statues

There are a number of statues, which are not idols in the classic sense, but have strong occult ties and overtones. These would include statues of wizards, trolls, demons, bats, serpents, witches, evil castles, ghosts and goblins, gremlins, and the like. This would include all types of tapestries that glorify evil or satanic practices as well.

All these types of statues should be removed from the home of Christians. It does not matter whether the statue is a cute version of a satanic creature; it should be destroyed and removed. One of the greatest deceptions is that cute things cannot be harmful. Remember, your home should be a place of safety and refuge, not a battleground. Your home should be safe for the weakest Christian to find shelter and comfort.

Occult Objects

The secular market place is filled with objects that have occult significance. These objects induct the unwary into Satan's realm and have no business in the home of the Christian. It is a false hope to believe that an unopened Bible on the shelf counteracts all heavily used occult objects. Below is a list of objects that are used to call upon Satan and his demonic hordes. They should not be treated lightly. Christians should not use, glamorize, or promote the occult in any way.

- Crystals (used for channeling power)
- Ouija boards
- Tarot cards

- Pyramids
- Pentagrams
- Good luck charms
- Amulets
- Egyptian worship symbols
- Talisman
- Astrology charts

Occult Jewelry

There is an abundance of jewelry with devils, dragons, bats, skulls, and other strong occult themes, which should be destroyed. There is no reason why a Christian should wear the marks of death and satanic bondage. Christians should proclaim in every area of life that they belong to the Lord Jesus Christ and have chosen to walk in the kingdom of light. There are certain types of jewelry, which are not occult in their form, but have been made for use in mystical or demonic religions. (This would include some American Indian jewelry.) This type of jewelry should not be owned or worn and should be destroyed.

Occult Books

There are many different types of occult books from New Age literature to the satanic bible, which should be removed from the house. These books detail practices of evil. They can also act as place of operation for oppressive evil spirits. If you believe a book, magazine, or article is satanic or evil, don't have it in your home. It doesn't matter that it is valuable. Get rid of it.

Pornography

This would include all types of pornography from soft core (airbrushed pictures of scantily-clad women) to hard core (graphic depictions of sexual relations). Pornography also includes written material, which contains no pictures, but describes sexuality or sexual acts in a seductive, alluring, immoral, or degenerate fashion. *(Let me be clear: pornography is a form of sexual assault and opens doorways that should stay closed.)*

Cult Books

There are many books produced, which are not overtly occult or demonic, but pervert the truth of God and the faith once delivered to the saints. Unless God has called you to a specific ministry of dealing with these groups, these books should not be in your home.

Music

There is a great debate about various types of music and its impact on Christians. Any music that arouses immoral, violent, or sinful desires is to be discarded. Any music that details satanic practices or offers praise to Satan or demons is to be discarded. Any music that captivates one's mind so that little room is left for meditation on the Scriptures and the Lord Jesus Christ is to be discarded. Everyone must examine every piece of music they listen to.

Journal of the Spiritual Exercises
Ridding Your House of Occult Objects

1. What I actually did:

2. **What happened when I did it?**

CLOSING SPIRITUAL DOORWAYS

3. How will I use this in the future?

EXERCISE #9

DISCONTINUING OCCULT PRACTICES

THE MOST OBVIOUS AREA TO RECEIVE DEMONIC ATTACHMENT OR DEMONIC OPPRESSION IS direct involvement in the occult. Each area of involvement in the occult should be brought before the Lord in confession, repentance, and renunciation. In the next section, there is a list of occult, cultic, and perversion practices. Check off the areas you have personally been involved in. Christians needs to cut themselves off spiritually from these practices and enter into full adoption in the family of God.

Check	Involvement in the Occult	Did you practice? How often?
	Occult practices	
	Astrology	
	Witchcraft	

CLOSING SPIRITUAL DOORWAYS

Check	Involvement in the Occult	Did you practice? How often?
	White Magic	
	Black Magic	
	Séances	
	Magical role-playing games	
	ESP	
	Clairvoyance	
	Medium	
	Spiritism	
	Second Sight	
	Mind Reading	
	Fortune Telling	
	Palm Reading	
	Tea Leaf Reading	
	Crystal Ball	
	Tarot Cards	
	Horoscopes	
	Reincarnation	
	Metaphysic Healings	
	Deep Hypnosis	

DISCONTINUING OCCULT PRACTICES

Check	Involvement in the Occult	Did you practice? How often?
	Curses, Hexes, Vexes	
	Spells	
	Charms	
	Oaths; Death, Blood...	
	Voodoo	
	Santeria	
	Levitation	
	Psychometry	
	Automatic Writing	
	Channeling	
	Numerology	
	Astral Projection	
	Occult Literature	
	Psychic Phenomena	
	Crystals	
	Pyramid Power	
	Pacts with the Devil	
	Sacrifices (ritual and actual)	
	Bride of Satan	

Check	Involvement in the Occult	Did you practice? How often?
	Para psychology	
	Religious Yoga	
	Transcendental Meditation	
	Spirit Guides	
	Ascended Masters	
	Ecstatic Utterance	
	Prophecy	
	Religious Acupuncture	
	Conversation with spirits	
	Black Mass	
	Mind Control	
	Death Magic	
	Free Masonry	
	Poltergeists	
	Psychic abilities	
	Satan Worship	
	Table Lifting	
	Speaking in trance	

DISCONTINUING OCCULT PRACTICES

Check	Involvement in the Occult	Did you practice? How often?
	Spiritist prophecy, soothsaying	
	Spiritistic magic	
	Transfiguration, Translocation, Materialization, Apports, Deports	
	Symbols of Occultic Peace: Egyptian Fertility, Pentagram, etc.	
	Vampires	
	Weleda Medicines	

A Prayer of Confession

This is a suggested prayer of confession. You do not have to use these exact words. But these ideas of confession, repentance, renunciation, cleansing, and transfer should be present. This is not a magical formula; it is a suggested prayer. It is your sincerity and honesty before God that is important. Also, in order for a prayer of confession to be maximally effective in breaking very powerful satanic strongholds and influence, it is best if this prayer is prayed out loud with a mature Christian brother or sister who is watching you pray and is praying with and for you.

CLOSING SPIRITUAL DOORWAYS

1. **Confession and Repentance (1 John 1:9: 2 Tim 2:24)**

    Lord Jesus, I agree with you that worshiping or serving another god is wrong. I turn away from it and ask that all the forgiveness that is in your death on Calvary be applied to my sin in this area. You say in your Word that all forms of witchcraft, worship of other gods, and seeking power for selfish ends through the spiritual world is wrong. I realize that only in your power and energy and through your direction can I successfully turn away from this sin.

2. **Renunciation (2 Cor 4:4)**

    I repudiate, reject, and renounce any ground, place, or power I gave to Satan in my life through my involvement in false worship or occult worship. I give to the Lord Jesus Christ all power over this area of my life. I willingly surrender this area to the Lord Jesus Christ and the Holy Spirit.

3. **Cleansing and Expulsion (1 John 1:9; Eph 4:27)**

    I cancel any contract I may have made with Satan through false worship or occult practice. I ask you, Lord Jesus, to cleanse me of any and all unrighteousness (including demons and demonic strongholds) because you say in your Word that "If we confess our sins He is faithful and just to forgive us our sins and to cleanse us of all unrighteousness." (1 John 1:9)

DISCONTINUING OCCULT PRACTICES

4. **Transfer of Ownership and Infusion of the Spirit of Truth (2 Cor 10:3-5; Col 1:27, 28; Eph 5:18)**

   I right now transfer ownership of all worship in my life to the Lord Jesus Christ. I choose to take every thought regarding spiritual power, other gods, and true worship captive to Christ (2 Cor 10:3-5) and allow Him full lordship in this area. I ask you, Lord Jesus, that you would fill this area of my life with the Holy Spirit of truth, so that I would be wise, thankful, and able to see your plan in this area in the future. Thank you, Lord Jesus, for dying on the cross for me. I choose to cooperate with you in the worship area of my life so that the process you began in me when I first trusted in you can continue. (Phil 1:6) I realize that you want to display through me your character qualities. (Col 1:27,28; Gal 2:20)

   In the Name and for the Glory of the Lord Jesus Christ, Amen

Journal of the Spiritual Exercises
Discontinuing Occult Practices

1. **What I actually did:**

2. What happened when I did it?

CLOSING SPIRITUAL DOORWAYS

3. How will I use this in the future?

CLOSING THE DOORWAY OF TRANSFERENCE

EXERCISE #10

TURNING TRANSFERENCE INTO SPIRITUAL FREEDOM

Exodus 34:7b

TRANSFERENCE REFERS TO ALL THE WAYS THAT DEMONIC SPIRITS TRANSFER AROUND A person. You might think of them hovering around you, waiting for you to step in the direction of a particular sin that you may be prone to do because an open doorway. Transference can occur to a person even if they themselves weren't specifically involved in a past sin. Because of generational sin, or something evil that happened to you in the past, you could be prone toward a specific sin. You probably have not committed a specific sin yet, but the demonic spirit's desire is to take advantage of your tendency toward that sin by causing you to act or to move toward the sin. It ultimately wants to have a greater measure of control over you. There are three areas (or doorways) that could produce a transference problem: ancestral sins, victimization, and curses.

Ancestral Sins

Any of the doorways we have discussed are potential portals to what are called "familiar spirits," in that they are familiar with your family and the type of sin that your family is most tempted by. Members of each generation must recognize that they are the inheritors of the good and bad from the previous generations. Each individual must deal with his or her tendencies and susceptibility to sin in certain areas. This would include family and cultural patterns of sin and immorality, which are accepted by the individual without even evaluating its morality.

Victimization

This is any abusive behavior, which is perpetrated upon the individual. This behavior is oppressive and is usually designed to establish or retain control over the person. It is not beneficial, but rather oppressive and destructive. It would include physical abuse, sexual abuse, emotional abuse, mental abuse, spiritual abuse, and even financial abuse.

Curses

Transference can occur through curses that are placed on a person, family, or object, which need to be canceled or destroyed, and the person, family, or object redeemed. These curses might include familiar spirits, oaths (blood, death), hexes, vows, curses, vexes, spells, charms, amulets, or psychic abilities taken out against or on the person, family, or object.

Four Steps to Deal with Transference Problems

Transference problems can be dealt with in four steps:
1. information
2. confession
3. repentance
4. infusion of truth

These four steps may have to be repeated a number of times as ever deeper layers are uncovered in this area of transference. Breaking free of these transferences often require multiple passes through the material. The individual takes a first pass through the material by spending time agreeing with God about God's standards. They should acknowledge that their relatives, friends, and others have participated in what was wrong and may have forced them to be a part of this behavior.

A second pass through this material sometime later may be helpful for many people. This would be done with a trusted mentor or someone who has done some educated probing. Then a third pass through this material may be made with the help of prayer warriors or safe family members. It can really help to agree with God that these behaviors that family, friends, or even the individual have been involved in were wrong. He or she is admitting that they were wrong and asking for the blood of Jesus to cover these sins. A final pass may be made through this material with the help of those who have the gifts of discernment of spirits and their spiritual eyes on these parts of a person's past.

The confession step (for transference) does not assume that the individual is taking personal responsibility for the sinful acts of his or her parents or grandparents but rather agreeing with God that those actions were wrong and damaging. It is powerful to acknowledge basic morality and orient yourself to what God says about immoral actions. It breaks the hold of that person, demon, or sin in one's life to be able to walk away from spiritual influences connected with those actions.

In order to fully be free from the attachments and oppression of past occult associations, it is often the most helpful to go back through all of your past involvements and confess these to the Lord Jesus Christ. Each one of these violations of God's laws is a confession item. Do not seek to bunch these together in a blanket confession. If it becomes hard to pray a prayer of confession over any them, you may need help praying through that material. Seek a spiritually mature brother or sister in Christ to pray with you or a prayer team.

Journal of the Spiritual Exercises
Turning Transference into Spiritual Freedom

1. What I actually did:

2. **What happened when I did it?**

TURNING TRANSFERENCE INTO SPIRITUAL FREEDOM

3. How will I use this in the future?

EXERCISE #11

ASSESSING SPIRITUAL AND MORAL HISTORY OF PARENTS, GRANDPARENTS, AND ANCESTORS

It is important for people who are experiencing spiritual oppression to understand how involved their parents, grandparents, and ancestors were in the occult and immorality. The following list is categorized into various areas of sin. This can be very informative about what potential things family members could have been involved in throughout history. Go through it and check what you know about your family's involvement. Understand that you are answering about your family, not yourself. Note what was done and who did it. Some of the practices listed might be confusing or new to you. If you do not know what something is, just skip it and move on. We will assume that if you do not know about it, your family did not practice it.

Involvement in Pride:

Check	Pride Sins	Who Practiced This?
	Pride—Inordinate Self-Focus	
	Arrogance—Superiority	
	Bigotry—Prejudice	
	Criticism—Cynical	
	Unteachable spirit	
	Lack of Self-Acceptance	

Involvement in Rebellion:

Check	Rebellion Sins	Who Practiced This?
	Unrighteous rebellion	
	Lack of submission	
	Rebellious Attitude—negative attitude toward authority	
	Lack of teamwork	

ASSESSING SPIRITUAL AND MORAL HISTORY

Check	Rebellion Sins	Who Practiced This?
	Lack of servant's heart	

Involvement in Lust and Adultery:

Check	Lust & Adultery Sins	Who Practiced This?
	Pornography	
	Mental adultery	
	Transvestitism	
	Adultery	
	Prostitution	
	Immoral conduct	
	Indecent exposure	
	Voyeurism	
	Masturbation	
	Sexual harassment	

Check	Lust & Adultery Sins	Who Practiced This?
	Premarital sexual encounters	
	Homosexual episodes	
	Incest	
	Bestiality	
	Satanic/ritual sexuality	

Involvement with Anger, Violence, and Murder:

Check	Anger, Violence, and Murder Sins	Who Practiced This?
	Outbursts of anger	
	Rage	
	Wrath	
	Burning resentment	
	Malice	

Check	Anger, Violence, and Murder Sins	Who Practiced This?
	Violence against others	
	Assault	
	Murder	

Involvement with Bitterness, Revenge, and Forgiveness:

Check	Bitterness, Revenge, and Forgiveness Sins	Who Practiced This?
	Bitterness	
	Revenge	
	Lack of forgiveness	
	Rejoicing in harm of others	
	Refusal to move on	

Involvement in the Occult:

Check	Occult Sins	Who Practiced This?
	Occult practices	
	Astrology	
	Witchcraft	
	White Magic	
	Black Magic	
	Séances	
	Magical role-playing games	
	ESP	
	Clairvoyance	
	Medium	
	Spiritism	
	Second Sight	
	Mind Reading	

ASSESSING SPIRITUAL AND MORAL HISTORY

Check	Occult Sins	Who Practiced This?
	Fortune Telling	
	Palm Reading	
	Tea Leaf Reading	
	Crystal Ball	
	Tarot Cards	
	Horoscopes	
	Reincarnation	
	Metaphysic Healings	
	Deep Hypnosis	
	Curses, Hexes, Vexes	
	Spells / Charms	
	Oaths; Death, Blood	
	Voodoo	
	Santeria	

CLOSING SPIRITUAL DOORWAYS

Check	Occult Sins	Who Practiced This?
	Levitation	
	Psychometry	
	Automatic Writing	
	Channeling	
	Numerology	
	Astral Projection	
	Occult Literature	
	Psychic Phenomena	
	Crystals	
	Pyramid Power	
	Pacts with the Devil	
	Sacrifices (ritual and actual)	
	Bride of Satan	
	Para psychology	

ASSESSING SPIRITUAL AND MORAL HISTORY

Check	Occult Sins	Who Practiced This?
	Religious Yoga	
	Transcendental Meditation	
	Ascended Masters	
	Ecstatic Utterance	
	Prophecy	
	Religious Acupuncture	
	Conversation with spirits	
	Black Mass	
	Mind Control	
	Death Magic	
	Free Masonry	
	Poltergeists	
	Psychic abilities	
	Queen of Darkness; Queen of black witches	

Check	Occult Sins	Who Practiced This?
	Satan Worship	
	Table Lifting	
	Speaking in trance	
	Spiritist prophecy, soothsaying	
	Transfiguration, Translocation, Materialization	
	Symbols of Occult Peace: Egyptian Fertility, Pentagram, etc.	
	Vampires	
	Weleda Medicines	
	Other Religions	

Review the list again and take note of your answers. Acknowledge in prayer that it was evil and against God's laws and desires. Even though you may not have committed them personally, confess that these sins were wrong in the sight of God. Complete the confession work sheet as an interested party, not the perpetrator of any sins that your family may have committed.

A Prayer of Confession

This is a suggested prayer of confession. You do not have to use these exact words. But these ideas of confession, repentance, renunciation, cleansing, and transfer should be present. This is not a magical formula; it is a suggested prayer. It is your sincerity and honesty before God that is important. Also, in order for a prayer of confession to be maximally effective in breaking very powerful satanic strongholds and influence, it is best if this prayer is prayed out loud with a mature Christian brother or sister who is watching you pray and is praying with and for you.

1. **Confession and Repentance (1 John 1:9; 2 Tim 2:24)**

   Lord Jesus, I agree with you that occult practice and false worship is wrong. I turn away from it and ask that all the forgiveness that is in your death on Calvary be applied to my sin and the sin of my family in this area. You say in your Word that all witchcraft and Satanism is wrong. I realize that only in your power and energy and through your direction can I successfully turn away from this sin.

2. **Renunciation (2 Cor 4:4)**

   I repudiate, reject, and renounce any ground, place, or power my relatives may have given to Satan in my life through their involvement in false worship or occult practices. I give to the Lord Jesus Christ all power over this area of my life. I willingly surrender this area to the Lord Jesus Christ and the Holy Spirit.

3. **Cleansing and Expulsion (1 John 1:9; Eph 4:27)**

   I cancel any contract they may have made with Satan through occult practices or false worship. I ask you, Lord Jesus, to cleanse me of any and all unrighteousness (including demons and demonic strongholds) because you say in your Word that "If we confess our sins, He is faithful and just to forgive us our sins and to cleanse us of all unrighteousness." (1 John 1:9)

4. **Transfer of Ownership and Infusion of the Spirit of Truth (2 Cor 10:3–5; Col 1:27, 28; Eph 5:18)**

   I right now transfer ownership of my worship to the Lord Jesus Christ. I choose to take every thought regarding worship and spiritual power captive to Christ (2 Cor 10:3–5) and allow Him full lordship in this area. I ask you, Lord Jesus, that you would fill this area of my life with the Holy Spirit of truth, so that I would be wise, thankful, and able to see your plan in this area in the future. Thank you, Lord Jesus, for dying on the cross for me. I choose to cooperate with you in this worship area of my life so that the process you began in me when I first trusted in you can continue. (Phil 1:6) I realize that you want to display through me your character qualities. (Col 1:27, 28; Gal 2:20)

   In the Name and for the Glory of the Lord Jesus Christ, Amen

Journal of the Spiritual Exercises
Assessing the Spiritual and Moral History of Parents, Grandparents, and Ancestors

1. **What I actually did:**

CLOSING SPIRITUAL DOORWAYS

2. What happened when I did it?

3. How will I use this in the future?

EXERCISE #12

FIGHTING VICTIMIZATION

VICTIMIZATION IS ANY BEHAVIOR WHICH IS ABUSIVE AND PERPETRATED UPON THE individual. This behavior is oppressive and is usually designed to establish or retain control over the person. It does not benefit the victim in any way, but instead is oppressive and destructive. It would include physical abuse, sexual abuse, emotional abuse, mental abuse, spiritual abuse, and even financial abuse.

A Prayer for Fighting Abuse

This is a suggested prayer of confession. You do not have to use these exact words. But these ideas of confession, repentance, renunciation, cleansing, and transfer should be present. This is not a magical formula; it is a suggested prayer. It is your sincerity and honesty before God that is important. Also, in order for a prayer of confession to be maximally effective in breaking very powerful satanic strongholds and influence, it is best if this prayer is prayed out loud with a mature Christian brother or sister who is watching you pray and is praying with and for you.

1. **Confession and Repentance (1 John 1:9; 2 Tim 2:24)**

   Lord Jesus, I agree with you that spiritual, physical, mental, emotional, sexual, vocational, or financial abuse is wrong. I ask for your power to overcome the damage that this abuse did in my life. I pray that you fill me with your forgiveness, justice, and power to move beyond what happened to me.

2. **Renunciation (2 Cor 4:4)**

   I repudiate, reject, and renounce any ground, place, or power my relatives may have given to Satan in my life through their abuse. I give to the Lord Jesus Christ all power over this area of my life. I willingly surrender this area to the Lord Jesus Christ and the Holy Spirit. I ask you to energize me to live a new life free from abuse.

3. **Cleansing and Expulsion (1 John 1:9; Eph 4:27)**

   I cancel any contract they may have made with Satan through the abuse that I suffered. I ask you, Lord Jesus, to cleanse me and fill me with your righteous power to live above the abuse of my past and embrace a life of real love.

4. **Transfer of Ownership and Infusion of the Spirit of Truth (2 Cor 10:3–5; Col 1:27, 28; Eph 5:18)**

   I right now transfer ownership of my abuse to the Lord Jesus Christ. I choose to take every thought regarding my abuse captive to Christ (2 Cor 10:3–5) and allow Him full lordship in this area. I ask you, Lord Jesus, that you would fill this area of my life with the Holy Spirit of truth, so that I would be wise, thankful, and able to see how you want to turn this evil into something good in my life and others. Thank you, Lord Jesus, for dying on the cross for me. I choose to cooperate with you so that the process you began in me when I first trusted in you can continue. (Phil 1:6) I realize that you to use my recovery as a unique testament to the Love of God and the character of Christ. (Col 1:27, 28; Gal 2:20)

Journal of the Spiritual Exercises
Fighting Victimization

1. What I actually did:

2. **What happened when I did it?**

CLOSING SPIRITUAL DOORWAYS

3. How will I use this in the future?

EXERCISE #13

BREAKING CURSES

ANOTHER AREA OF TRANSFERENCE IS ANY curse placed on a person, family, or object. These curses need to be canceled or destroyed and the person, family, or object redeemed. These curses might include familiar spirits, oaths (blood, death, other), hexes, vows, curses, vexes, spells, charms, amulets, or psychic abilities taken out against or on the person, family, or object.

A Prayer for Fighting Curses

This is a suggested prayer of confession. You do not have to use these exact words. But these ideas of confession, repentance, renunciation, cleansing, and transfer should be present. This is not a magical formula; it is a suggested prayer. It is your sincerity and honesty before God that is important. Also, in order for a prayer of confession to be maximally effective in breaking very powerful satanic strongholds and influence, it is best if this prayer is prayed out loud with a mature Christian brother or sister who is watching you pray and is praying with and for you.

1. **Confession and Repentance (1 John 1:9; 2 Tim 2:24)**

   Lord Jesus, I agree with you that familiar spirits, oaths (blood, death, other), hexes, vows, curses, vexes, spells, charms, amulets, and psychic abilities are wrong. I turn away from these and ask that only the power of God, which comes baptized in the blood of the Lord Jesus Christ, is a part of my life.

2. **Renunciation (2 Cor 4:4)**

   I repudiate, reject, and renounce any ground, place, or power my relatives may have given to Satan in my life through familiar spirits, oaths (blood, death, other), hexes, vows, curses, vexes, spells, charms, amulets, or psychic abilities. I give to the Lord Jesus Christ all power over any familiar spirits, oaths (blood, death, other), hexes, vows, curses, vexes, spells, charms, amulets, and psychic abilities. I willingly surrender this area to the Lord Jesus Christ and the Holy Spirit.

3. **Cleansing and Expulsion (1 John 1:9; Eph 4:27)**

   I cancel any contract they may have made with Satan through familiar spirits, oaths (blood, death, other), hexes, vows, curses, vexes, spells, charms, amulets, and psychic abilities. I ask you, Lord Jesus, to cleanse me of any and all familiar spirits, oaths, (blood, death, other), hexes, vows, curses, vexes, spells, charms, amulets, and psychic abilities.

4. **Transfer of Ownership and Infusion of the Spirit of Truth (2 Cor 10:3-5; Col 1:27, 28; Eph 5:18)**

   I right now transfer ownership of all blessing, energy, position, and power in my life to the Lord Jesus Christ. I choose to take every thought, any blessing, energy, position, and power in my life captive to Christ (2 Cor 10:3-5) and allow Him full lordship in this area. I ask you, Lord Jesus, that you would fill this area of my life with the Holy Spirit of truth, so that I would be wise, thankful, and able to see your plan in this area in the future. Thank you, Lord Jesus, for dying on the cross for me. I choose to cooperate with you so that the process you began in me when I first trusted in you can continue. (Phil 1:6) I realize that you want to display through me your character qualities. (Col 1:27, 28; Gal 2:20)

   In the Name and for the Glory of the Lord Jesus Christ, Amen

CLOSING SPIRITUAL DOORWAYS

Journal of the Spiritual Exercises
Breaking Curses

1. What I actually did:

2. **What happened when I did it?**

CLOSING SPIRITUAL DOORWAYS

3. How will I use this in the future?

CONCLUSION

Closing the seven spiritual doorways can have huge, positive effects in your life. You will be freed up to love others with new joy. You will be able to more easily understand and follow God's will for your life. I would encourage you to reach up and access the spiritual world through the work of Christ on the cross. Jesus has done all that is needed for us to access the spiritual world in a positive and non-destructive way. Practice the spiritual disciplines to draw close to the Lord God Almighty through the guidance of the Holy Spirit and the finished work of the Lord Jesus Christ.

HOW TO USE THIS BOOK

There are five ways that this material was designed for use. Originally, it was to be used as an Intensive Discipleship material for small groups of men or women to help them move significantly forward in their Christian life. It can also be used for a personal devotion, mentor-directed study, a class format, or a sermon series with small groups. I have outlined how this could be conducted.

Small Group Study

1. Ask three to five people join you in doing this study. Participate in a small groups program within your church in which people are assigned to your small group to cover this material, or develop your own group.

2. Set aside an hour or so each week (or each month) to do the three crucial things required for spiritual life-change. First, discuss what happened when you practiced the spiritual exercises in the previous lesson. Second, learn about the next set of exercises and information. Third, take personal prayer requests from each member. This can often be the most effective if it is done at breakfast or lunch in a

restaurant before or during the workday. It doesn't have to be at church. In fact, many times it is better if it is not.

3. The time should be divided into three sections.

   a. The first 20-30 minutes should be spent sharing what happened when each person practiced the spiritual exercises that were assigned. Everyone must share, even if they do not think that they were successful.

   b. The second 10-30 minutes are spent in learning the next week or month's lessons and exercises.

   c. The final 10-30 minutes are spent taking prayer requests from everyone. The prayer requests must be about the person themselves. This is not the time to have the group pray for a family member.

4. Each member of the group can read the book for further understanding of the information and exercises. The time spent together is not primarily a presentation time.

5. If one or more of the people have not tried or mastered the exercises, then the leader should feel free to repeat the same lesson again and again until this spiritual exercise is mastered.

6. If the group is meeting monthly rather than weekly, then more exercises are assigned. It can be helpful to have some form of accountability set up to make

HOW TO USE THIS BOOK

sure people are working on the exercises. This may be a daily or weekly e-mail stating what exercise they tried. The full explanation will come in the group time; but if everybody e-mails or texts what they are doing then everybody stays on track.

Let's take a look at the first small group meeting:

1. Let everyone introduce themselves. A sixty-second bio is usually helpful and lets everyone get to know everyone else.

2. Open in prayer.

3. Introduce the topic that you will be exploring and pass out the books. Give an overview of the whole series.

4. Explain the first week or month's exercises.

5. Save 10-20 minutes for personal prayer requests.

The key to an effective discipleship group is not what the teacher says; it is what the disciple does. Give each person lots of time to tell about what happened when he or she started to practice the discipline. If the people in the group did not adequately try the discipline or did not see results from trying the discipline, then spend another week on that discipline. The goal of the group is not to get through the material within a specific amount of time, but to develop new spiritual habits that will change their lives.

Personal Devotional Study

A second way to use this material is as a personal devotional study. In this format, you can work through the material and look up the verses on your own, taking notes, practicing the exercises, and writing down your experiences for personal review. In this type of study, proceed at your own pace. It may be one chapter a week or one chapter a day. The key is that the information is digested and the exercises are tried until some level of mastery is accomplished. It can be helpful to share your progress in this material with a mentor or spiritual accountability partner. Let's take a look at what a personal devotional study would look like.

1. Open in prayer.

2. Read the material in the chapter.

3. Practice the exercise(s) suggested.

4. Record what you did, what happened when you did it, and what you continue to do because of using this exercise.

5. Practice the exercise again or in a different way until mastery.

Mentor Directed Study

One of the most powerful ways of using this material is to ask a respected Christian you know to mentor you through this material. They do not need to do the study with you, but they do need to monitor and encourage you in the process of this study.

HOW TO USE THIS BOOK

1. Ask a mentor to listen to your progress through this material once a month and pray for you as you explore these issues and exercises.

2. Meet the first time with your mentor and purchase a book for them so they can be tracking your progress. This meeting could be at a restaurant or a coffee house so that the meeting is more informal.

    a. Let them know what you are hoping to accomplish with this study and at what speed you would like to move through the material.

    b. Give them the freedom to teach, correct, rebuke and train you as you move through the material. (2 Tim 3:16)

    c. Agree to meet monthly or weekly to hear updates on how you are doing. Remember, this is about you not about them. They are mentoring you through this material and may not be going through it themselves. They are your spiritual guide not a co-laborer.

    d. Have your mentor watch you pray or practice the exercise as they watch. They may be able to suggest ways to more effectively practice the spiritual exercise.

3. Ask your mentor to follow the following format for your monthly or weekly sessions.

   a. Spend 20-30 minutes listening to what you have done and experienced as you have worked through the exercises.

   b. Listen to their insights and additions.

   c. Spend 10-20 minutes of them assigning and exploring the next chapter or reassigning the current material because they think there is a need to dwell on these ideas or habits more thoroughly.

   d. Spend 10-20 minutes giving the mentor three specific personal prayer requests you would like them to pray for until the next meeting.

Realize that your mentor may want to move off in tangents that are not directly tied to the material in this study guide, but that is what you want. They have life experience and spiritual wisdom that you want to be poured into your life. A mentor can often see mistakes or missteps that are about to take place when we cannot see them. Also, mentors can listen for the emotional, psychological, or spiritual pain that we have not been able to talk about before.

Class Format

A fourth way to use this material is in a class or mid-week teaching time at the church. The material that is contained in the book can be presented to a class, but it should take only about half the time allowed for the class. The other half of the time should be used for small groups to discuss what happened the week before when the discipline was tried. Also allow for questions and prayer requests in regard to a growing spiritual life. This material should be repeated regularly as a part of a church's ongoing discipleship strategy. Every year or every other year, a church can run one of these classes so that people are moving forward.

The greatest danger to using this material in a class setting is that the teacher will use the whole time to present the material, not allowing adequate discussion of what happened when it was tried.

Second, there is the danger that it will be offered as new information only rather than as new practices or habits to incorporate into their life. The value of this material is in the exercises, not in the information. It is not possible to have a consistently deep walk with God without some of these disciplines being a part of their life. These materials are not just for delivering new information; they are to be practiced.

A third danger in using this material in a classroom setting is that the teacher or facilitator may not feel the freedom to repeat a discipline until all in the class have adequately tried it. There needs to be the freedom to go back over material that is not fully embraced until it has been adequately explored.

Let's take a look at what using this material in a classroom setting would look like.Advertise the class in various places at church, work, or community. For the first class, let's take a look at what the first meeting of the classroom setting would look like:

1. Open in prayer.
2. Introduce an overview of the topic and pass out the books.
3. Let people know that this is an exercise/application focused group, not a new information focused group. They will learn new information, but only so that they can then apply it to their life.
4. Introduce the first few exercises that will be tried in the first week or month.
5. Break the group into small groups for personal prayer requests.

For the remaining class periods, the following is the format for the standard meeting.

1. Open in prayer.
2. Give people 10-30 minutes to break into small groups of three or four and tell each other how the exercises from the last meeting went.
3. Spend 10-30 minutes explaining the new concepts and exercises to the group.
4. Put the group back into their small groups for personal prayer requests. Everybody has to share something that they want everyone to pray about.

Sermon Series and Small Groups

A fifth way to use this material is as a sermon series with accompanying small groups. This is where the whole church listens to the sermon series that the pastor is preaching, and then all small groups practice the material by doing the spiritual workouts at the end of each chapter. This is really a lab-lecture model of discipleship. It can be quite effective if the small group allows people to talk about trying the various disciplines. This is a way to jump-start Sunday morning attenders into people who are serious about developing spiritual habits. This multi-pronged approach can be very effective if there is adequate planning and opportunity for new groups to form even after the sermon series has started.

The goal of this book is that many Christians will begin practicing their Christianity and experiencing new levels of closeness with God. The process of walking with Christ takes time. The addition of new habits of life is essential. Expect that some will try these disciplines and then stop. Expect that others will have been waiting for this material for a long time and can quickly push to new depths with God. Patiently persevere; you and others will reap great joy in the presence of God.

ABOUT THE AUTHOR

D R. GIL STIEGLITZ IS AN AUTHOR, SPEAKER, CATALYST, PROFESSOR, PASTOR, COUNSELOR, and leadership consultant. He speaks to thousands of people every year about building healthy and successful relationships. Gil currently serves as Discipleship Pastor at Bayside Church, a dynamic multi-site church on the north side of Sacramento, CA. He served for five years as Executive Pastor of Adventure Christian Church in Roseville, CA. He is an adjunct professor at Western Seminary (Sacramento Campus), a church consultant for Thriving Churches International, and Founder and President of Principles To Live By, a discipleship and publishing non-profit dedicated to equipping people, pastors, and churches to live out God's best for them. He has served on the board of a number of non-profit groups to help start churches, revitalize pastors, and rescue minors from sex trafficking and exploitation. He has been a denominational executive for thirteen years with the Evangelical Church of America and was the senior pastor at a mid-sized church in Southern California for seventeen years. Gil has a heart for helping people become all that God wants them to be. He believes that a "Great Life Is Great Relationships." To learn more about Gil, his books, resources, and speaking and consulting opportunities, visit www.ptlb.com.

MORE RESOURCES FROM PRINCIPLES TO LIVE BY

Books

Becoming a Godly Husband
Becoming Courageous
Breakfast with Solomon, Volumes 1 - 3
Breaking Satanic Bondage
Deep Happiness: Eight Secrets
Delighting in God
Delighting in Jesus
Developing a Christian Worldview
God's Radical Plan for Wives
God's Radical Plan for Wives Companion Bible Study
Going Deep in Prayer: Forty Days of In-Depth Prayer
Keeping Visitors
Leading a Thriving Ministry
Marital Intelligence
Mission Possible: Winning the Battle over Temptation
Proverbs: Devotional Commentary, Volumes 1 - 2
Satan and the Origin of Evil
Secrets of God's Armor
Spiritual Disciplines of a C.H.R.I.S.T.I.A.N.
The Gift of Seeing Angels and Demons: A Handbook for Discerners of Spirits
The Keys to Grapeness—Growing a Spirit-led Life
The Schemes of Satan
They Laughed When I Wrote Another Book about Prayer, Then They Read It
Touching the Face of God: Forty Days of Adoring God

Uniquely You: A Faith-Driven Journey to Your True Identity and Water-Walking, Giant-Slaying, History-Making Destiny
Weapons of Righteousness Study Guides
Why There Has to Be a Hell

Online Video Courses

Mission Possible: Winning the Battle over Temptation
Becoming a Godly Husband
The Keys to Grapeness—Growing a Spirit-led Life

Audio Files

Becoming a Godly Parent
Becoming a Godly Husband
Biblical Meditation: Keys of Transformation
Deep Happiness: Eight Secrets
Everyday Spiritual Warfare Series
God's Guide to Handling Money
Marital Intelligence: Battling for Your Marriage
Intensive Spiritual Warfare Series
Spiritual War Surrounding Money
The Four Keys to a Great Family
The Ten Commandments
Raising Your Leadership Level: Double Your Impact
Spiritual Warfare: Using the Weapons of God to Win Spiritual Battles
Weapons of Righteousness Series

www.PTLB.com

www.ingramcontent.com/pod-product-compliance
Lightning Source LLC
LaVergne TN
LVHW051600070426
835507LV00021B/2677